Boston Red Sox 2019

A Baseball Companion

Edited by Patrick Dubuque, Aaron Gleeman and Bret Sayre

Baseball Prospectus

Craig Brown and Dave Pease, Consultant Editors
Rob McQuown and Harry Pavlidis, Statistics Editors

Copyright © 2019 by DIY Baseball, LLC.
All rights reserved

This book or any part thereof may not be reproduced or transmitted in any form or by any means, electronic or mechanical, including photocopying, recording, or by any information storage and retrieval system, without permission in writing from the publisher.

Limit of Liability/Disclaimer of Warranty: While the publisher and the author have used their best efforts in preparing this book, they make no representations or warranties with respect to the accuracy or completeness of the contents of this book and specifically disclaim any implied warranties of merchantability or fitness for a particular purpose. No warranty may be created or extended by sales representatives or written sales materials. The advice and strategies contained herein may not be suitable for your situation. You should consult with a professional where appropriate. Neither the publisher nor the author shall be liable for any loss of profit or any other commercial damages, including but not limited to special, incidental, consequential, or other damages.

Library of Congress Cataloging-in-Publication Data:
paperback
ISBN-13: 978-1-949332-02-5

Project Credits
Cover Design: Kathleen Dyson
Interior Design and Production: Jeff Pease, Dave Pease
Layout: Jeff Pease, Dave Pease

Baseball icon courtesy of Uberux, from https://www.shareicon.net/author/uberux

Ballpark diagram courtesy of Lou Spirito/THIRTY81 Project, https://thirty81project.com/

Manufactured in the United States of America
10 9 8 7 6 5 4 3 2 1

Table of Contents

Foreword v
   Rob Mains

Statistical Introduction vii

Part 1: Team Analysis

Table for Two: Previewing the 2019 Boston Red Sox 3
   Ben Carsley and Alexis Collins

Performance Graphs 7

2018 Team Performance 8

2019 Team Projections 9

Team Personnel 10

Fenway Park Stats 11

Red Sox Team Analysis 13

Part 2: Player Analysis

Red Sox Player Analysis 20

Red Sox Prospects 97

Part 3: Featured Articles

The Hole in The Shift is Fixing Itself 109
   Russell Carleton

The State of the Quality Start 113
   Rob Mains

Heads-Up Hacking—The First Pitch 119
   Matthew Trueblood

A Hymn for the Index Stat 125
   Patrick Dubuque

Index of Names 129

Foreword

Rob Mains

Welcome to this companion of the 2019 Boston Red Sox. We at Baseball Prospectus are excited to provide this analysis of the Red Sox.

Our website, Baseball Prospectus, is a leader in delivering high-quality commentary and data to baseball fans everywhere. To some, those words—commentary and data—appear mutually exclusive. There are people out there who believe that traditional analysis and advanced analytics must run on different paths. But the simplistic narrative of stats vs. traditionalists just isn't true. Every team's analytics department interacts with scouting, development, and major league operations with a common goal: Delivering a championship. New technologies, like radar tracking of pitch speeds and movement, enable talent evaluators to focus on qualitative aspects of pitching like mechanics and pitch sequencing. In-game strategies like infield shifts, based on batters' hit tendencies, help turn balls in play into outs. Hitters use information to adjust their swings to maximize run production.

All these numbers can seem, at best, intimidating, and at worst, counterproductive to the casual fan. Even as technology and analysis have embedded themselves deeply into the way teams run, it can often feel like statistics create a displacement between the viewer and the sport, breaking them out of the action. And yet every fan incorporates the numbers to some degree; stats like batting average and earned run average, so fundamental to how we talk about performance, are actually complicated formulas. They don't bother people because those formulas have become second nature, as easy to translate as the action on the field.

Along the way, new statistics have entered baseball's lexicon. You'll see some of them, like on-base percentage (which measures a batter's ability to get on base via walk, hit batter, or hit), OPS (on-base plus slugging), and average exit velocity (the speed of balls off a hitter's bat) on broadcasts. Others, like DRC+, might well be new to you. Some of them have been well-defined to the public, others haven't. That lack of context has created ambiguity. Fans know that a ball hit 100 mph is scorched, but does that mean extra bases? (Not if it's hit on the ground or high in the air it doesn't.)

For those who are amenable to them, the new statistics can increase the enjoyment and understanding of the game. They can help fans identify when a pitcher is tiring, when a stolen base or a bunt attempt makes sense (and, more often, when it doesn't), or how a team's lineup might be constructed. Websites like Baseball Prospectus add to that understanding by weaving metrics into the narrative of the game. That's the goal of this publication: to take some of the newer, more complicated statistics and make them as intuitive as the ones on the back of old baseball cards.

But you don't need to love analytics to love baseball. The fans at BP who worked together to write this guide are captivated first and foremost by the game itself. We're drawn to Aaron Judge's power, Francisco Lindor's glove, Billy Hamilton's speed and Patrick Corbin's slider and don't need numbers to tell us why they're so mesmerizing. The underlying statistics provide depth to the game that we all love.

We hope you'll find that this guide helps you better understand the Red Sox. Our analysts have studied the team's major league personnel and its minor league affiliates to identify their strengths and weaknesses, both the obvious ones and those that only a careful dissection of players' performances—yes, including the data—can reveal. You don't need us to tell you who was good and who wasn't in 2018, but our models and writers can help you project how each player is going to perform this year and beyond, and appreciate the greatness of each new game as it unfolds. As in the sport itself, the human and analytic components combine to generate a deeper overall understanding.

Think back to the first time you saw a baseball game on a high-definition TV. You'd grown familiar with how the game looked and felt on a picture tube. But new TV allowed you to see details that you'd never seen before. That's how advanced statistics work. The game itself is why you're here and why you're buying this. (And, for that matter, why we wrote it.) The statistical measures provide the sharper focus, the detail, the depth of knowledge that you didn't have before, generating an overall superior picture. Enjoy the view.

—*Rob Mains is an author of Baseball Prospectus.*

Statistical Introduction

Sports are, fundamentally, a blend of athletic endeavor and storytelling. Baseball, like any other sport, tells its stories in so many ways: in the arc of a game from the stands or a season from the box scores, in photos, or even in numbers. At Baseball Prospectus, we understand that statistics don't replace observation or any of baseball's stories, but complement everything else that makes the game so much fun.

What stats help us with is with patterns and precision, variance and value. This book can help you learn things you may not see from watching a game or hundred, whether it's the path of a career over time or the breadth of the entire MLB. We'd also never ask you to choose between our numbers and the experience of viewing a game from the cheap seats or the comfort of your home; our publication combines running the numbers with observations and wisdom from some of the brightest minds we can find. But if you *do* want to learn more about the numbers beyond what's on the backs of player jerseys, let us help explain.

Offense

At the end of this past year, we've revised our methodology for determining batting value. Long-time readers of Baseball Prospectus will notice that we've retired True Average in favor of a new metric: Deserved Runs Created Plus (DRC+). Developed by Jonathan Judge and our stats team, this statistic measures everything a player does at the plate–reaching base, hitting for power, making outs, and moving runners over–and puts it on a scale where 100 equals league-average performance. A DRC+ of 150 is terrific, a DRC+ of 100 is average, and a DRC+ of 75 means you better be an excellent defender.

DRC+ also does a better job than any of our previous metrics in taking contextual factors into account. The model adjusts for how the park affects performance, but also for things like the talent of the opposing pitcher, value of different types of batted-ball events, league, temperature, and other factors. It's able to describe a player's expected offensive contribution than any other statistic we've found over the years, and also does a better job of predicting future performance as well.

The other aspect of run-scoring is baserunning, which we quantify using Baserunning Runs. BRR not only records the value of stolen bases (or getting caught in the act), but also accounts for a runner's ability to go first to third on a single or advance on a fly ball.

Defense

Where offensive value is *relatively* easy to identify and understand, defensive value is ... not. Over the past dozen years, the sabermetric community has focused mostly on stats based on zone data: a real-live human person records the type of batted ball and estimated landing location, and models are created that give expected outs. From there, you can compare fielders' actual outs to those expected ones. Simple, right?

Unfortunately, zone data has two major issues. First, zone data is recorded by commercial data providers who keep the raw data private unless you pay for it. (All the statistics we build in this book and on our website use public data as inputs.) That hurts our ability to test assumptions or duplicate results. Second, over the years it has become apparent that there's quite a bit of "noise" in zone-based fielding analysis. Sometimes the conclusions drawn from zone data don't hold up to scrutiny, and sometimes the different data provided by different providers don't look anything alike, giving wildly different results. Sometimes the hard-working professional stringers or scorers might unknowingly inflict unconscious bias into the mix: for example good fielders will often be credited with more expected outs despite the data, and ballparks with high press boxes tend to score more line drives than ones with a lower press box.

Enter our Fielding Runs Above Average (FRAA). For most positions, FRAA is built from play-by-play data, which allows us to avoid the subjectivity found in many other fielding metrics. The idea is this: count how many fielding plays are made by a given player and compare that to expected plays for an average fielder at their position (based on pitcher ground-ball tendencies and batter handedness). Then we adjust for park and base-out situations.

When it comes to catchers, our methodology is a little different thanks to the laundry list of responsibilities they're tasked with beyond just, well, catching and throwing the ball. By now you've probably heard about "framing" or the art of making umpires more likely to call balls outside the strike zone for strikes. To put this into one tidy number, we incorporate pitch tracking data (for the years it exists) and adjust for important factors like pitcher, umpire, batter, and home-field advantage using a mixed-model approach. This grants us a number for how many strikes the catcher is personally adding to (or subtracting from) his pitchers' performance ... which we then convert to runs added or lost using linear weights.

Framing is one of the biggest parts of determining catcher value, but we also take into account blocking balls from going past, whether a scorer deems it a passed ball or a wild pitch. We use a similar approach–one that really benefits from the pitch tracking data that tells us what ends up in the dirt and what doesn't. We also include a catcher's ability to prevent stolen bases and how well they field balls in play, and *finally* we come up with our FRAA for catchers.

Pitching

Both pitching and fielding make up the half of baseball that isn't run scoring: run prevention. Separating pitching from fielding is a tough task, and most recent pitching analysis has branched off from Voros McCracken's famous (and controversial) statement, "There is little if any difference among major-league pitchers in their ability to prevent hits on balls hit in the field of play." The research of the analytic community has validated this to some extent, and there are a host of "defense-independent" pitching measures that have been developed to try and extricate the effect of the defense behind a hurler from the pitcher's work.

Our solution to this quandry is Deserved Run Average (DRA), our core pitching metric. DRA looks like earned run average (ERA), the tried-and-true pitching stat you've seen on every baseball broadcast or box score from the past century, but it's very different. To start, DRA takes an event-by-event look at what the pitchers does, and adjusts the value of that event based on different environmental factors like park, batter, catcher, umpire, base-out situation, run differential, inning, defense, home field advantage, pitcher role, and temperature. That mixed model gives us a pitcher's expected contribution, similar to what we do for our DRC+ model for hitters and FRAA model for catchers. (Oh, and we also consider the pitcher's effect on basestealing and on balls getting past the catcher.)

It's important to note that DRA is set to the scale of runs allowed per nine innings (RA9) instead of ERA, which makes DRA's scale slightly higher than ERA's. The reason for this is because ERA tends to overrate three types of pitchers:

1. Pitchers who play in parks where scorers hand out more errors. Official scorers differ significantly in the frequency at which they assign errors to fielders.
2. Ground-ball pitchers, because a substantial proportion of errors occur on grounders.
3. Pitchers who aren't very good. Better pitchers often allow fewer unearned runs than bad pitchers, because good pitchers tend to find ways to get out of jams.

Since the last time you picked up an edition of this book, we've also made a few minor changes to DRA to make it better. Recent research into "tunneling"–the act of throwing consecutive pitches that appear similar from a batter's point of view until after the swing decision point–data has given us a new contextual factor to account for in DRA: plate distance. This refers to the distance between successive pitches as they approach the plate, and while it has a smaller effect than factors like velocity or whiff rate, it still can help explain pitcher strikeout rate in our model.

New Pitching Metrics for 2019

We're including a few "new" pitching metrics for 2019's suite of Baseball Prospectus publications, but you may be familiar with them if you've spent time scouring the internet for stats.

Fastball Percentage

Our fastball percentage (FB%) statistic measures how frequently a pitcher throws a pitch classified as a "fastball," measured as a percentage of overall pitches thrown. We qualify three types of fastballs:

1. The traditional four-seam fastball;
2. The two-seam fastball or sinker;
3. "Hard cutters," which are pitches that have the movement profile of a cut fastball and are used as the pitcher's primary offering or in place of a more traditional fastball.

For example, a pitcher with a FB% of 67 throws any combination of these three pitches about two-thirds of the time.

Whiff Rate

Everybody loves a swing and a miss, and whiff rate (WHF) measures how frequently pitchers induce a swinging strike. To calculate WHF, we add up all the pitches thrown that ended with a swinging strike, then divide that number by a pitcher's total pitches thrown. Most often, high whiff rates correlate with high strikeout rates (and overall effective pitcher performance).

Called Strike Probability

Called Strike Probability (CSP) is a number that represents the likelihood that all of a pitcher's pitches will be called a strike while controlling for location, pitcher and batter handedness, umpire and count. Here's how it works: on each pitch, our model determines how many times (out of 100) that a similar pitch was called for a strike given those factors mentioned above, and when normalized for each batter's strike zone. Then we average the CSP for all pitches thrown by a pitcher in a season, and that gives us the yearly CSP percentage you see in the stats boxes.

As you might imagine, pitchers with a higher CSP are more likely to work in the zone, where pitchers with a lower CSP are likely locating their pitches outside the normal strike zone, for better or for worse.

Projections

Many of you aren't turning to this book just for a look at what a player has done, but for a look at what a player is going to do: the PECOTA projections. PECOTA, initially developed by Nate Silver (who has moved on to greater fame as a political analyst), consists of three parts:

1. Major-league equivalencies, which use minor-league statistics to project how a player will perform in the major leagues;
2. Baseline forecasts, which use weighted averages and regression to the mean to estimate a player's current true talent level; and
3. Aging curves, which uses the career paths of comparable players to estimate how a player's statistics are likely to change over time.

With all those important things covered, let's take a look at what's in the book this year.

Team Prospectus

You bought this book to learn more about your favorite (or maybe least-favorite, who are we to judge?) team, so let's talk about them. After a thoughtful preview of the 2019 season, you'll be presented with our Team Prospectus. This outlines many of the key statistics for each team's 2018 season, as well as a very inviting stadium diagram.

First you'll find the Performance Graphs page. The first is the 2018 Hit List Ranking. This shows our Hit List Rank for the team on each day of the 2018 season and is intended to give you a picture of the ups and downs of the team's season, including their highest and lowest ranks of the year. Hit List Rank measures overall team performance and drives the Hit List Power Rankings at the baseballprospectus.com website.

The second graph is Committed Payroll and helps you see how the team's payroll has compared to the MLB and divisional average payrolls over time. Payroll figures are currents as of January 1, 2019; with so many free agents still unsigned as of this writing, the final 2018 figure will likely be significantly different for many teams. (In the meantime, you can always find the most current data at Baseball Prospectus' Cot's Baseball Contracts page.)

The third graph is Farm System Ranking and displays how the Baseball Prospectus prospect team has ranked the organization's farm system since 2007. It also indicates the highest and lowest ranks that the farm system achieved over that time.

We start the Team Performance page with the squad's unadjusted and third-order 2018 win-loss records, presented in divisional context. We then list the three highest performing hitters and pitchers by WARP for 2018. Beneath that are a host of other team statistics. **Pythag** presents an adjusted 2018 winning percentage, calculated by taking runs scored per game (**RS/G**) and runs allowed per game (**RA/G**) for the team, and running them through a version of Bill James' Pythagorean formula that was refined and improved by David Smyth and Brandon Heipp. (The formula is called "Pythagenpat," which is equally fun to type and to say.)

Next up is **DRC+**, described earlier, to indicate the overall hitting ability of the team either above or below league-average. Run prevention on the pitching side is covered by **DRA** (also mentioned earlier) and another metric: Fielding Independent Pitching (**FIP**), which calculates another ERA-like statistic based on strikeouts, walks, and home runs recorded. Defensive Efficiency Rating (**DER**) tells us the percentage of balls in play turned into outs for the team, and is a quick fielding shorthand that rounds out run prevention.

After that, we have several measures related to roster composition, as opposed to on-field performance. **B-Age** and **P-Age** tell us the average age of a team's batters and pitchers, respectively. **Salary** is the combined team payroll for all on-field players, and Doug Pappas' Marginal Dollars per Marginal Win (**M$/MW**) tells us how much money a team spent to earn production above replacement level.

Ending this batch of statistics is the number of disabled list days a team had over the season (**DL Days**) and the amount of salary paid to players on the disabled list (**$ on DL**); this final number is expressed as a percentage of total payroll.

Next to each of these stats, we've listed each team's MLB rank in that category from 1st to 30th. In this, 1st always indicates a positive outcome and 30th a negative outcome, except in the case of salary–1st is highest.

The Team Projections page is intended to convey the team's operational capacity entering the 2019 season. We start with the team's PECOTA projected record for 2019, again in divisional context. The **+/-** column indicates how many more or less wins the team is projected to get than they got in 2018. We then list the three highest projected hitters and pitchers by WARP for 2018. A brief farm system summary follows, with the team's top prospect and number of BP Top 101 Prospects. Finally, we list the key new players and departed players, along with their 2019 projected WARP.

Alex Bregman 3B

Born: 03/30/94 Age: 25 Bats: R Throws: R
Height: 6'0" Weight: 180 Origin: Round 1, 2015 Draft (#2 overall)

YEAR	TEAM	LVL	AGE	PA	R	2B	3B	HR	RBI	BB	K	SB	CS	AVG/OBP/SLG
2016	CCH	AA	22	285	54	16	2	14	46	42	26	5	3	.297/.415/.559
2016	FRE	AAA	22	83	17	6	0	6	15	5	12	2	1	.333/.373/.641
2016	HOU	MLB	22	217	31	13	3	8	34	15	52	2	0	.264/.313/.478
2017	HOU	MLB	23	626	88	39	5	19	71	55	97	17	5	.284/.352/.475
2018	HOU	MLB	24	705	105	51	1	31	103	96	85	10	4	.286/.394/.532
2019	HOU	MLB	25	675	96	38	3	23	78	73	107	12	4	.272/.359/.463

Breakout: 6% Improve: 52% Collapse: 5% Attrition: 2% MLB: 100%
Comparables: Anthony Rendon, David Wright, Pablo Sandoval

YEAR	TEAM	LVL	AGE	PA	DRC+	VORP	BABIP	BRR	FRAA	WARP
2016	CCH	AA	22	285	172	38.9	.286	1.6	SS(51): -3.4, 3B(11): 1.4	2.7
2016	FRE	AAA	22	83	161	10.0	.333	-1.2	SS(14): 2.1, LF(3): -0.1	0.8
2016	HOU	MLB	22	217	107	9.6	.317	0.5	3B(40): 0.9, SS(6): -0.1	1.1
2017	HOU	MLB	23	626	114	34.7	.311	-1.5	3B(132): 8.7, SS(30): -2.9	3.9
2018	HOU	MLB	24	705	150	72.6	.289	-1.6	3B(136): 5.4, SS(28): -0.4	7.4
2019	HOU	MLB	25	675	125	37.3	.295	0.0	3B 7, SS 0	4.6

After the projections page, we share a few items about the team's home ballpark. There's the aforementioned diagram of the park's dimensions (including distances to the outfield wall), a few important biographical facts about the stadium, a graphic showing the height of the wall from the left-field pole to the right-field pole, and a table showing three-year park factors for the stadium. The park factors are displayed as indexes where 100 is average, 110 means that the park inflates the statistic in question by 10 percent, and 90 means that the park deflates the statistic in question by 10 percent.

Following the ballpark page, we have a **Personnel** section that lists many of the important decision-makers and upper-level field and operations staff members for the franchise, as well as any former Baseball Prospectus staff members who are currently part of the organization.

Position Players

After all that information and a thoughtful bylined essay covering each team, we present our player comments. Each player is listed with the major-league team who employed him as of early January 2019. If a player changed teams after that point via free agency, trade, or any other method, you'll be able to find them in the book for their previous squad.

First, we cover biographical information (age is as of June 30, 2019) before moving onto the stats themselves. Our statistic columns include standard identifying information like **YEAR**, **TEAM**, **LVL** (level of affiliated play) and **AGE** before getting into the numbers. Next, we provide raw, unstranslated numbers like you might find on the back of your dad's baseball cards: **PA** (plate appearances), **R** (runs), **2B** (doubles), **3B** (triples), **HR** (home runs), **RBI** (runs batted in), **BB** (walks), **K** (strikeouts), **SB** (stolen bases) and **CS** (caught stealing). Then we have unadjusted "slash" statistics: **AVG** (batting average), **OBP** (on-base percentage) and **SLG** (slugging percentage).

Just below the stats box is **PECOTA** data, which is discussed further in a following section. After that, it's on to a pithy and always-informative comment written by a member of the Baseball Prospectus staff, before we cover more stats.

The second text box repeats YEAR, TEAM, LVL, AGE, and PA, then moves on to **DRC+** (Deserved Runs Created Plus), which we described earlier as total offensive expected contribution compared to the league average. Next, one of our oldest active metrics, **VORP** (Value Over Replacement Player), considers offensive production, position and plate appearances. In essence, it is the number of runs contributed beyond what a replacement-level player at the same position would contribute if given the same percentage of team plate appearances. VORP does not consider the quality of a player's defense.

BABIP (batting average on balls in play) tells us how often a ball in play fell for a hit, and can help us identify whether a batter may have been lucky or not ... but note that high BABIPs also tend to follow the great hitters of our time, as well as speedy singles hitters who put the ball on the ground.

The next item is **BRR** (Baserunning Runs), which covers all of a player's baserunning accomplishments which includes (but isn't limited to) swiped bags and failed attempts. Next is **FRAA** (Fielding Runs Above Average), which also includes the number of games previously played at each position noted in parentheses. Multi-position players have only their two most frequent positions listed here, but their total FRAA number reflects all positions played.

Our last column here is **WARP** (Wins Above Replacement Player). WARP estimates the total value of a player, which means for hitters it takes into account hitting runs above average (calculated using the DRC+ model), BRR and FRAA. Then, it makes an adjustment for positions played and gives the player a credit for plate appearances based upon the difference between "replacement level"¬-which is derived from the quality of players added to a team's roster after the start of the season¬-and the league average.

Catchers

Catchers are a special breed, and thus they have earned their own separate box which displays some of the defensive metrics that we've built just for them. As an example, let's check out J.T. Realmuto.

YEAR	TEAM	P. COUNT	FRM RUNS	BLK RUNS	THRW RUNS	TOT RUNS
2016	MIA	18935	-8.5	1.8	2.1	-5.6
2017	MIA	18959	5.3	1.7	1.0	9.1
2018	MIA	16399	-0.4	0.9	0.1	0.4
2019	PHI	18448	-1.4	1.5	0.7	0.8

The **YEAR** and **TEAM** columns match what you'd find in the other stat box. **P. COUNT** indicates the number of pitches thrown while the catcher was behind the plate, including swinging strikes, fouls, and balls in play. **FRM RUNS** is the total run value the catcher provided (or cost) his team by influencing the umpire to call strikes where other catchers did not. **BLK RUNS** expresses the total run value above or below average for the catcher's ability to prevent wild pitches and passed balls. **THRW RUNS** is calculated using a similar model as the previous two statistics, and it measures a catcher's ability to throw out basestealers but also to dissuade them from testing his arm in the first place. It takes into account factors like the pitcher (including his delivery and pickoff move) and baserunner (who could be as fast as Billy Hamilton or as slow as Yonder Alonso). **TOT RUNS** is the sum of all of the previous three statistics.

Pitchers

Let's give our pitchers a turn, using 2018 NL Cy Young winner Jacob deGrom as our example. Take a look at his first stat block: the first line and the **YEAR**, **TEAM**, **LVL** and **AGE** columns are the same as in the position player example earlier.

Here too, we have a series of columns that display raw, unadjusted statistics compiled by the pitcher over the course of a season: **W** (wins), **L** (losses), **SV** (saves), **G** (games pitched), **GS** (games started), **IP** (innings pitched), **H** (hits allowed) and **HR** (home runs allowed). Next we have two statistics that are rates: **BB/9** (walks per nine innings) and **K/9** (strikeouts per nine innings), before returning to the unadjusted **K** (strikeouts).

Next up is **GB%** (ground ball percentage), which is the percentage of all batted balls that were hit in the ground, including both outs and hits. Remember, this is based on observational data and subject to human error, so please approach this with a healthy dose of skepticism.

BABIP (batting average on balls in play) is calculated using the same methodology as it is for position players, but it often tells us more about a pitcher than it does a hitter. With pitchers, a high BABIP is often due to poor defense or bad luck, and can often be an indicator of potential rebound, and a low BABIP may be cause to expect performance regression. (A typical league-average BABIP is close to .290-.300.)

After a witty 150ish words on the player like only Baseball Prospectus's staff can provide, it's on to that second stat block, which repeats the YEAR, TEAM, LVL, and AGE columns. The metrics **WHIP** (walks plus hits per inning pitched) and **ERA** (earned run average) are old standbys: WHIP measures walks and hits allowed on a per-inning basis, while ERA measures earned runs on a nine-inning basis. Neither of these stats are translated or adjusted.

DRA (Deserved Run Average) was described at length earlier, and measures how many runs the pitcher "deserved" to allow per nine innings. Please note that since we lack all the data points that would make for a "real" DRA for minor-league events, the DRA displayed for minor league partial-seasons is based off of different data. (That data is a modified version of our cFIP metric, which you can find more information about on our website.)

Jacob deGrom RHP
Born: 06/19/88   Age: 31   Bats: L   Throws: R
Height: 6'4"   Weight: 180   Origin: Round 9, 2010 Draft (#272 overall)

YEAR	TEAM	LVL	AGE	W	L	SV	G	GS	IP	H	HR	BB/9	K/9	K	GB%	BABIP
2016	NYN	MLB	28	7	8	0	24	24	148	142	15	2.2	8.7	143	47%	.312
2017	NYN	MLB	29	15	10	0	31	31	201[1]	180	28	2.6	10.7	239	48%	.305
2018	NYN	MLB	30	10	9	0	32	32	217	152	10	1.9	11.2	269	48%	.281
2019	NYN	MLB	31	13	9	0	31	31	186	145	18	2.3	10.7	221	46%	.286

Breakout: 8%   Improve: 29%   Collapse: 28%   Attrition: 6%   MLB: 85%
Comparables: Erik Bedard, A.J. Burnett, CC Sabathia

YEAR	TEAM	LVL	AGE	WHIP	ERA	DRA	WARP	MPH	FB%	WHF	CSP
2016	NYN	MLB	28	1.20	3.04	3.30	3.5	96.3	59.6	12.1	47.2
2017	NYN	MLB	29	1.19	3.53	3.02	5.7	97.2	55.5	14.5	49.5
2018	NYN	MLB	30	0.91	1.70	2.09	8.0	98.2	52.1	16.3	48.4
2019	NYN	MLB	31	1.02	2.91	3.23	3.9	96.6	54.5	14.8	48.2

Just like with hitters, **WARP** (Wins Above Replacement Player) is a total value metric that puts pitchers of all stripes on the same scale as position players. We use DRA as the primary input for our calculation of WARP. You might notice that relief pitchers (due to their limited innings) may have a lower WARP than you were expecting or than you might see in other WARP-like metrics. WARP does not take leverage into account, just the actions a pitcher performs and the expected value of those actions ... which ends up judging high-leverage relief pitchers differently than you might imagine given their prestige and market value.

MPH gives you the pitcher's 95th percentile velocity for the noted season, in order to give you an idea of what the *peak* fastball velocity a pitcher possesses. Since this comes from our pitch tracking data, it is not publicly available for minor-league pitchers.

Finally, we display the three new pitching metrics we described earlier. **FB%** (fastball percentage) gives you the percentage of fastballs thrown out of all pitches. **WhiffRt** (whiff rate) tells you the percentage of swinging strikes induced out of all pitches. **CS Prob** (called strike probability) expresses the likelihood of all pitches thrown to result in a called strike, after controlling for factors like handedness, umpire, pitch type, count, and location.

PECOTA

All players have PECOTA projections for 2019, as well as a set of other numbers that describe the performance of comparable players according to PECOTA. All projections for 2019 are for the player at the date we went to press in early January and are projected into the league and park context as indicated by the team abbreviation. All PECOTA projected statistics represent a player's projected major-league performance.

The numbers beneath the player's stats–Breakout, Improve, Collapse, Attrition–are part and parcel of the PECOTA projections. They estimate the likelihood of changes in performance relative to the player's previously-established level of production, based on the performance of comparable players:

Breakout Rate is the percent change that a player's production will improve by at least 20 percent relative to the weighted average of his performance over his most recent seasons.

Improve Rate is the percent chance that a player's production will improve at all relative to his baseline performance. A player who is expected to perform just the same as he has in the recent past will have an Improve Rate of 50 percent.

Collapse Rate is the percent chance that a position player's production will decline by at least 25 percent relative to his baseline performance.

Attrition Rate operates on playing time rather than performance. Specifically, it measures the likelihood that a player's playing time will decrease by at least 50 percent relative to his established level.

Breakout Rate and Collapse Rate can sometimes be counterintuitive for players who have already experienced a radical change in performance level. It's also worth noting that the projected decline in a player's rate performances might not be indicative of an expected decline in underlying ability or skill, but could just be an anticipated correction following a breakout season.

MLB% is the percentage of similar players who played in the major leagues in their relevant season.

The final pieces of information are the player's three highest-scoring comparable players as determined by PECOTA. All comparables represent a snapshot of how the listed player was performing at the same age as the current player, so if a 23-year-old pitcher is compared to Bartolo Colon, he's actually being compared to a 23-year-old Colon, not the version that pitched for the Rangers in 2018, nor to Colon's career as a whole.

Boston Red Sox 2019

A few points about pitcher projections. First, we aren't yet projecting peak velocity, so that column will be blank in the PECOTA lines. Second, projecting DRA is trickier than evaluating past performance, because it is unclear how deserving each pitcher will be of his anticipated outcomes. However, we know that another DRA-related statistic–contextual FIP or cFIP–estimates future run scoring very well. So for PECOTA, the projected DRA figures you see are based on the past cFIPs generated by the pitcher and comparable players over time, along with the other factors described above.

Lineouts

In each chapter's Lineouts section, you'll find abbreviated text comments, as well as most of same information you'd find in our full player comments. We limit the stats boxes in this section to only including the 2018 information for each player.

Exclusive Player Visualizations

In our constant battle to provide you with new and interesting baseball content you can't find anywhere else, we've added a trio of data visualizations to each hitter's entry in these books and a pair of visualizations for each pitcher.

For hitters, you'll find three new infographics. The first is each player's **Batted Ball Distribution**, which displays the five major sections of the field: LF (left), LCF (left center), CF (center), RCF (right center), and RF (right). The percentage indicated tells us what percentage of batted balls from that hitter fell within that part of the field during the 2018 season. We've also included the hitter's slugging percentage on balls in play (also called **SLGCON**) for that part of the field.

You'll also see two heatmaps: **Strike Zone vs LHP** and **Strike Zone vs RHP**. These heat maps represent a view of the strike zone from behind the catcher. Areas where there is a darker coloration represent the places where a higher percentage of pitches resulted in hits. In other words, the heatmap represents a hitter's "sweet spots" for getting hits against either left-handed or right-handed pitchers, depending on the image.

Pitchers get two images that help explain what their pitches look like from a hitter's perspective: **Pitch Shape vs LHH** and **Pitch Shape vs RHH**. These images show you the shape and the "tunneling" effect of each pitcher's offerings from the batter's perspective. For each type of pitch that a pitcher throws (represented by an indicator shape), there's a set of dots indicating the flight path, where each dot represents a 0.01-second interval. This maps the average trajectory and speed of an offering, ending where the ball crosses the plate. The solid black box represents the regular strike zone, while the gray contour lines indicate the range of locations that a pitcher typically works in.

Below the image, we provide a bit more detailed information about each pitcher's average offering in the **Pitch Types** box. Here, we also list each of the pitcher's major offerings under the **Type** column.

- **Fastballs** (which usually refers to the four-seam variation)
- **Sinkers** and/or two-seam fastballs
- **Cutters** (which could include "hard" cutters like cut fastballs and "soft" cutters that resemble hard sliders)
- **Changeups** (not including most splitters)
- **Splitters** (split-fingered pitches, forkballs, and some split-changes)
- **Sliders** and/or slurves
- **Curveballs** (including spike-curveballs and knuckle-curveballs, as well as some slurvy curves)
- **Slow curveballs** and/or eephus pitches
- **Knuckleballs**
- **Screwballs**

The **Freq** column indicates the percentage of overall pitches that fall into each of those type categories; if a pitcher has a 16.55% score for changeups, then that's the percent of all pitches that he throws as changeups. **Velo** is exactly what you think it is: the average miles per hour for each pitch type. **H Mov** is the number of inches of horizontal movement on the average pitch of that type, while **V Mov** is the number of inches of vertical movement on the average pitch of that type. (At Baseball Prospectus, we measure this over the long flight of the ball and include gravity into the V Mov number in order to give you the most realistic representation of what the pitch *actually* does.)

If you're wondering about the second number in brackets, that's the index for that velocity or movement compared to the league average. Like DRC+, a score of 100 means that the speed or movement is about the same as league average, while a higher score means that there's higher velocity or movement than the league average. Numbers below 100 indicate less velocity or movement than the league average.

Part 1: Team Analysis

Table for Two: Previewing the 2019 Boston Red Sox

Ben Carsley and Alexis Collins

BEN CARSLEY: Can I just say how nice it is to be writing about the Red Sox with a Collins who knows what they're talking about? This is a big change for me.

ALEXIS COLLINS: Well, funny you should mention that, because Matt was one of the first people I found on Twitter when I wanted to learn more about the Red Sox. I will do my best to represent those Collinses who came before me.

BEN: Well you certainly can't do any worse! So let's start with the most obvious talking point—the Sox's rather stagnant offseason, Nate Eovaldi/Steve Pearce reunions aside. How well do you feel Dave Dombrowski and co. did given their aims?

ALEXIS: The Red Sox headed into the offseason knowing some of their biggest arms would be free agents, most notably Craig Kimbrel. The question was not whether Kimbrel was looking for a long-term deal, but if the Red Sox would make an offer. With the farm pretty bare, the team didn't have a lot to offer via trade, and the team's priority was clearly keeping the core intact. I expected Dombrowski to be aggressive seeking additional bullpen relief, but I suspect the luxury tax looms large: Instead he's signed a few lesser known arms (Dan Runzler, Brian Ellington, and Jenrry Mejia, known mainly for his suspensions). Kimbrel is still out there, but the team is making it look like they want an internal option to fill that closer role.

BEN: Yeah. I think the rest of the roster is in pretty terrific shape, but rolling into the season with Ryan Brasier and Matt Barnes as your two best relievers is… not great! You mentioned a bunch of the external Quad-A-type relievers Dombrowski brought in this offseason, and I'm sure they're hoping one or two of those guys click. Personally, I think any bullpen help is more likely to come from down on the farm. Durbin Feltman was a highish 2018 draft pick who lots of people felt could've held his own going straight to the majors, and he has set-up man upside. Travis Lakins finally moved to the bullpen and pitched very well there. Josh Taylor is already piquing some interest since he throws 98-plus. Darwinzon Hernandez and/or Michael Shawaryn could move quickly if transitioned to the pen. There are some interesting names here, but ideally you don't want to bank on performance from these types—you want to treat anything from this lot as found money, a la Brasier last year.

ALEXIS: So the bullpen is getting the most attention, but another ongoing conversation heading into the offseason was what to do about the three catchers on the major league roster. Would the team look to trade one of them or consider trying Swihart at another position (again)? This seems to bother people outside of the organization more than the Red Sox—credit to Alex Cora and his staff to somehow keeping all of them happy, although I guess winning a World Series will keep anyone happy! I'm not sure the tri-catcher strategy is a long-term solution, so I would expect by mid-season one of them becomes part of a trade for bullpen help.

BEN: It took me a long time to throw in the towel on Swihart, but I'm there. I don't expect him to be a meaningful MLB contributor anymore, at least not on a contender. The roster flexibility he provides is nice in theory, but I'd be much more willing to move on from him if faced with a roster crunch that at any previous point. As for Vazquez and Leon, well, I think the Sox are hoping for a (relative) offensive bounceback for the latter, while the former just is who he is. They don't need to hit much to justify their roster spots because they're so good defensively and the Sox's lineup is so loaded, but they *do* need to hit better as a duo than they did last year—among catchers with at least 100 at-bats, Vazquez finished 55th and Leon 65th in DRC+. That is beyond atrocious. I know the staff loves Leon, and I'm all for not fixing things that aren't broken, but one wonders how much better Boston could've been signing, say, Yasmani Grandal and moving Vazquez to a backup role.

ALEXIS: They would've been better at the plate, that's for sure. The third and final question heading into the offseason was who would end up playing second base for the Sox in 2019? Would the team bring Kinsler back, would Pedroia finally be healthy enough to make a significant contribution, or would they have to look for a replacement? With Kinsler signing a two-year, $8 million contract with the Padres, the Red Sox seemed to make the choice to stick with Pedroia at least for next season, with Eduardo Nunez, Brock Holt and Tzu-Wei Lin as backups.

BEN: Did you see the way Kinsler ran the bases last October? I'm fine with him playing on the other side of the country. The Sox's plan at second base may not be awe-inspiring, but I think they can cobble together 2-4 WAR between Pedroia, Nunez and Holt. I just hope Cora doesn't try to bat Pedroia or any of these guys near the top of the order when healthy; that time has passed.

Ok, so on to happier topics. The 2018 Red Sox enjoyed breakout performances from guys like Brasier, Barnes and Xander Bogaerts, who I am now contractually obligated to mention is extremely handsome. Who is your team's breakout player for 2019?

ALEXIS: The focus on Rafael Devers last season centered around his poor defensive after he led the AL with 24 errors. While his defense struggled a lot last season, Cora continued to work with him and show him that he believed in him. Offensively he has continued to display power at the plate, finishing last season with 21 home runs. Devers was only 21 last season and he knew what he needed to work on going into the offseason, so we should be able to tell pretty quickly if he put in the work.

BEN: Devers is a good one. Since I can't choose Bogaerts anymore, I'm gonna hop on the Eduardo Rodriguez train once again. Talent has never been the issue with Ed; it's always been health, and there's some irony in that the first good arm the Sox have developed in forever keeps having leg issues. Before Rodriguez hurt his ankle last season he had a 3.44 ERA and 110 strikeouts in 104.2 IP, and the Sox went 16-3 in the games he started. After the injury? E-Rod allowed 15 earned runs in 25 innings. He's good enough to be the No. 3 starter on a World Series-winning team. Hopefully this is the year he's healthy enough to serve as such.

Let's be honest—this team doesn't need a *ton* of improvement. They won 108 games last year and they're coming back pretty much exactly as-is minus Kimbrel and Joe Kelly, who our metrics had pegged as worth 1.5 WARP in 2018. That being said, we can't expect Bogarts, Betts and Bentinedi to all be as dominant as they were last year. The rotation also has more than its fair share of health risks in Sale, Rodriguez, Eovaldi and Price.

So even if the additions are marginal, how do you think this team will be improved by the end of the year?

ALEXIS: The biggest area of opportunity for improvement is the bullpen. While some of the current arms have the potential to improve on past performance, I'm not sure they will be able carry the load for the entire season. Ultimately, I think this will come down to the playoff race and where the team sits after the All-Star break. Dombrowski somewhat famously didn't make a move to improve the pen last July, and to the surprise of many, it worked out. Staying put likely won't be a luxury he has again this year, especially if the pen struggles in the first half or if Boston finds itself in a dog fight with New York, as we all expect.

BEN: The bullpen is the obvious call, yeah, but unfortunately I think the Red Sox are truly going to do everything they can to stay under the luxury tax threshold. Arguably their three best players—Betts, Sale and Bogaerts—will all be free agents in the next 24 months. The organization's top priority has to be extending Betts. In my opinion, Bogaerts shouldn't be far behind. I'm not adverse to extending Sale either, but the medicals there give me pause. Assuming Dombrowski wants to retain all three, the Sox are going to be pretty limited in the types of contracts they can acquire throughout the season. I don't see any talented, big-money guys walking through that door, and the Sox lack the prospects to trade for any good young/cheap players.

So I think roster improvements will come from small moves. A middle reliever or old closer, a la Brad Ziegler two years ago. A veteran backup at a position of need that emerges, a la Kinsler and Pearce last season. I think that's all we'll see, if anything.

ALEXIS: I agree the Red Sox won't be grabbing too many headlines for roster moves this season, and we can only hope any players added contribute as much as Kinsler and Pearce; those guys set some high expectations last year.

Focusing on what all Red Sox fans want to know, how will this team end up, and what kind of path will they take to get there? What are the chances the Red Sox repeat as World Series Champs?

BEN: So I think the Red Sox are very clearly one of the three-or-so best teams in baseball. The problem is that the very best team in baseball may be the Yankees now, and the Astros still scare the hell out of me. I'd expect those Big Three to be battling it out in October once again. For what it's worth, PECOTA has the Yankees finishing with 96 wins and the Red Sox with 89. While I agree with our projection system that New York is probably better on paper right now, I have no idea how PECOTA has the Sox dropping 19 wins with the same exact team, minus Kimbrel. This must be what it feels like to be a Royals fan. I'd peg the Sox as a low-to-mid-90s-win team. I'll be Extremely Scientific and say 94 wins.

ALEXIS: I think the Red Sox have enough talent to make another deep run into the postseason, but their success will ultimately come down to the bullpen and managing injuries. I expect Martinez and Betts to continue to carry the load offensively, with Bogarts and Benintendi contributing heavily. If they can score runs as easily as they did last season, that will give the bullpen some room for error. If the Red Sox advance to the League Championship series they will need similar luck to beat the Astros again to get to the World Series. With Cora at the helm, anything is possible!

BEN: Anything is possible, and one thing is certain: once the Sox "only" win like 94 games this year, Twitter Eggs and WEEI listeners will be calling for Cora's head, because Boston!

Performance Graphs

2018 Hit List Ranking

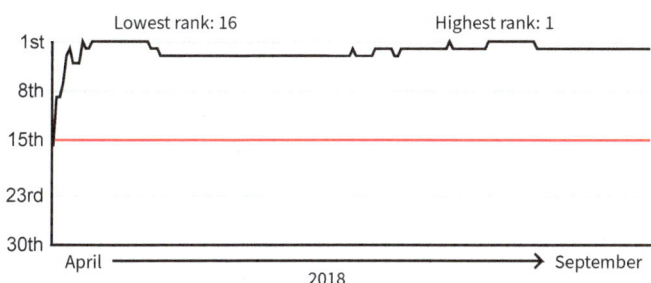

Committed Payroll (in millions)

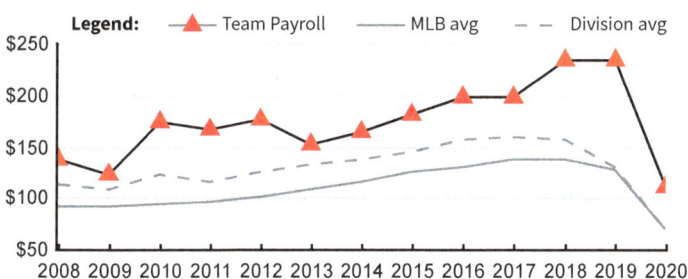

Farm System Ranking

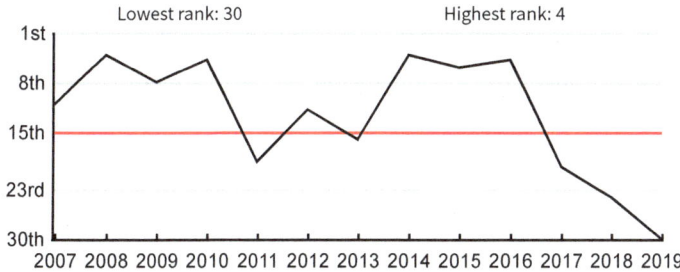

2018 Team Performance

ACTUAL STANDINGS

Team	W	L	Pct
BOS	**108**	**54**	**.666**
NYA	100	62	.617
TBA	90	72	.555
TOR	73	89	.450
BAL	47	115	.290

THIRD-ORDER STANDINGS

Team	W	L	Pct
NYA	99	63	.611
BOS	**99**	**63**	**.611**
TBA	98	64	.604
TOR	70	92	.432
BAL	54	108	.333

TOP HITTERS

Player	WARP
Mookie Betts	8.9
J.D. Martinez	6.3
Xander Bogaerts	4.9

TOP PITCHERS

Player	WARP
Chris Sale	5.6
David Price	3.2
Rick Porcello	2.8

VITAL STATISTICS

Statistic Name	Value	Rank
Pythagenpat	.640	2nd
Runs Scored per Game	5.41	1st
Runs Allowed per Game	3.99	5th
Deserved Runs Created Plus	112	1st
Deserved Run Average	4.18	10th
Fielding Independent Pitching	3.85	6th
Defensive Efficiency Rating	.706	15th
Batter Age	27.7	12th
Pitcher Age	28.9	20th
Salary	$233.2M	1st
Marginal $ per Marginal Win	$3.7M	17th
Disabled List Days	$1,259.0M	18th
$ on DL	11%	6th

2019 Team Projections

PROJECTED STANDINGS

Team	W	L	Pct	+/-
NYA	96	66	.592	-4
BOS	**90**	**72**	**.555**	**-18**
TBA	85	77	.524	-5
TOR	76	86	.469	+3
BAL	57	105	.351	+10

TOP PROJECTED HITTERS

Player	WARP
Mookie Betts	7.2
J.D. Martinez	5.1
Andrew Benintendi	3.4

TOP PROJECTED PITCHERS

Player	WARP
Chris Sale	5.4
Rick Porcello	2.3
David Price	2.2

FARM SYSTEM REPORT

Top Prospect	Number of Top 101 Prospects
Bobby Dalbec, unranked	0

KEY DEDUCTIONS

Player	WARP
Ian Kinsler	0.9
Hanley Ramirez	0.4
Joe Kelly	0.4
Drew Pomeranz	0.4

KEY ADDITIONS

Player	WARP
Gorkys Hernandez	0.9

Team Personnel

President, Baseball Operations
Dave Dombrowski

Senior VP/Assistant General Manager
Brian O'Halloran

Senior VP/Assistant General Manager
Eddie Romero

Manager
Alex Cora

BP Alumni
Todd Gold

Fenway Park Stats

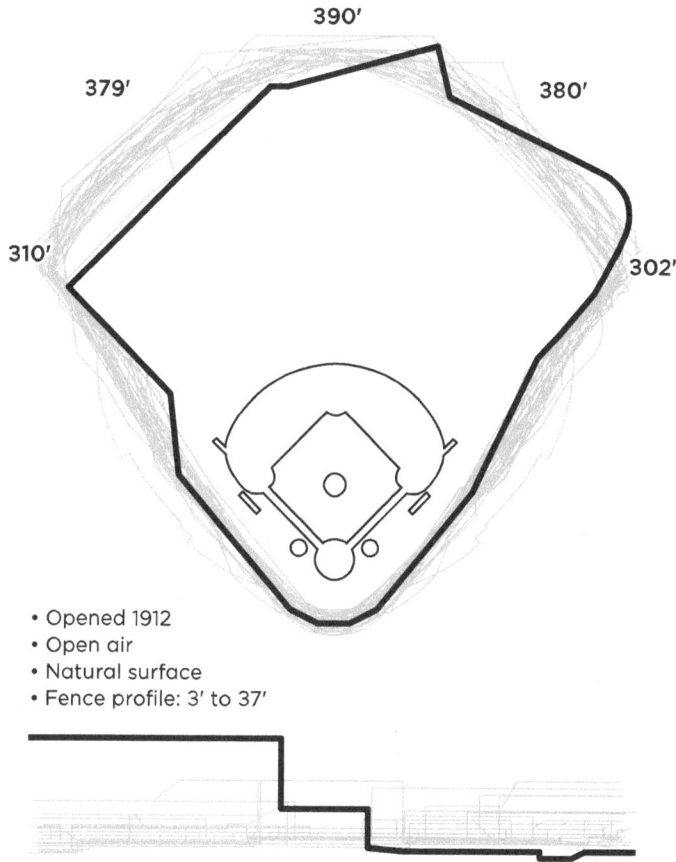

- Opened 1912
- Open air
- Natural surface
- Fence profile: 3' to 37'

Three-Year Park Factors

Runs	Runs/RH	Runs/LH	HR/RH	HR/LH
105	107	101	102	90

Red Sox Team Analysis

The culture of Red Sox fandom was going to change for the so-much-better after the affirming events of October 2004. Hell yeah, it was. How could it not? Though so many sunny summers that inevitably chilled to anguished autumns during the franchise's 86-season World Series championship drought, the daydream of what life as a Boston baseball fan would be like if—no, when, for there was always at least a frayed thread of authentic hope—the Red Sox won a World Series was a constant one.

The years when all the Boston faithful had were dreams provided a vivid idea of what winning would be like, how catharsis and pure, life-changing joy would feel, before it finally and at last came to be. There would be sweet camaraderie among us, an irresistible turn toward tender sentimentality, a warm this-is-for-you nostalgia for friends and loved ones who didn't live long enough to see their beloved Red Sox win, or for the beloved Sox players themselves who couldn't quite get it done despite their valiance. (Namely: Yaz.) Also, we would definitely stop bitching about every minute thing that went wrong, or even hinted that it might. Man, were we ever master pre-bitchers. No more of that. The good times, as the ubiquitous Neil Diamond earworm played during every eighth inning at Fenway, win or lose, told us, never would be so good. (So good.)

Yessir, that's how it was supposed to go, those 15 years ago, after the 2004 Red Sox—a united, supremely talented, oblivious-to-pressure squad, or one possessing every attribute necessary to exorcise all perceived ghosts and lame narratives—showed us what a seemingly impossible dream looked like once fulfilled. It has not gone that way, despite three more Red Sox champions since, and eight more among New England's other major professional sports teams since the turn of the century. Oh, for a time it did, and we were chill and satisfied and appreciative. For a time when it seemed like there would be a multiyear grace period before fans would ever have a gripe or a woe-is-us mentality. That grace period lasted … well, maybe through that 2004-05 winter, but it was long over by the time Red Sox fans began booing '04 postseason stalwart Keith Foulke in his injury-plagued summer of '05.

As exasperating as it can be, and as much as we should be accountable for our own actions as fans, I should stop suggesting that this is entirely on a vocal, negative segment of the fanbase because it is not entirely all their fault. It's the media culture that perpetuates it, shapes a bitter narrative, finds the negative needle a haystack of positives, conjures some negative conjecture when there is no real negative to be found, and then processes into hot takes for easy consumption.

I say this as a member of the media with the Marriott points to prove it. It's on us. And never more so than during the 2018 Red Sox season.

In retrospect, the '18 Red Sox played as close to a drama-free season of baseball excellence as there can be. They had the best record in spring training, sprinted out to a 17-2 regular-season start, never lost more than three games in a row, never won fewer than 15 games in a month, captured the American League East title by eight games, collected a franchise-record 108 regular season wins, and tore through the postseason, going 11-3 in the playoffs and World Series while wiping out the Yankees, Astros, and Dodgers along the way. The only team that has won more games and a World Series in a single season is the 1998 Yankees.

History will remember the 2018 Red Sox as one of the greatest teams ever. But few high-profile opinion makers in Boston—particularly in the aural cesspool that is sports radio—acknowledged it in real time. The most consistent talking points during the regular season weren't about Betts's all-around brilliance on a daily basis, rookie manager Alex Cora's charming candor and informed tactical boldness, or how J.D. Martinez was in every way the replacement for David Ortiz they so desperately lacked in 2017. No, they howled about Dave Dombrowski's checkered history of bullpen construction and his perceived failures to bolster the roster at the trade deadline. They told us time and time again that the regular season meant nothing, as if it were foolish and even wrong to enjoy the Red Sox' daily feats.

And they yapped about David Price. Everything about David Price that could be construed in the negative. His ignominious postseason history, his affinity for Fortnite, and his chronic struggles in New York.

I've often thought David Ortiz is the best thing ever to happen to the Red Sox; he delivered the big hits that all the legends before him could not. But Price, with his talent, defensiveness, flaws, and salary, might have been the greatest gift to happen to the Boston media. Much of the poison-tipped criticism aimed his way since signing a seven-year, $217 million free-agent deal with the Red Sox in December 2015 was earned. In his first two seasons, he brooded when he pitched poorly, carried himself with a sarcastic defiance on the occasions when he lived up to his ability and contract, and picked some strange battles to fight in what seemed a genuine but misguided quest to lead.

In June 2017, Price verbally ambushed Hall of Fame pitcher and Red Sox broadcaster Dennis Eckersley on the team plane, berating him for an innocuous comment he'd made about pitcher Eduardo Rodriguez's ugly pitching line during a rehab start. (Eck, ever candid, saw the line on a graphic and offered a one-word assessment: "Yuck.") Price later said Eckersley—who spent 24 years in the majors, endured two divorces, including one when his wife left him for a teammate, underwent alcohol rehabilitation, and was unfathomably gracious even after difficult on-field moments such as Kirk Gibson's home run in Game 1 of the 1988 World Series—didn't understand how hard it was to succeed in the major leagues. It was a jarring case-study in obliviousness.

But Price's latest failing—whether real or exaggerated—was too often the main story, when the real news was the unprecedented success of the ballclub; it's the first time I can recall seeing a dominating team also have a scapegoat.

The sports radio banshees didn't care to acknowledge that the Red Sox were cutting a path to history for a simple reason: preaching misery is lucrative. Negativity is proven to earn massive ratings in sports radio's targeted men 25-54 demographic in Boston, and with ratings come the coveted advertising dollars from every hair-replacement, weight-loss, and erectile dysfunction remedy hawker imaginable. Say this: They do know their audience.

One station, which happens to be the Red Sox radio rights holder, had internal discussions at the management level about turning its game broadcasts into more of a talk-show format. Imagine that. A broadcast booth that was once the home to Curt Gowdy, Ken Coleman, Ned Martin, and Jon Miller felt its broadcast might be enhanced by adding verbal fart-fest of contrived opinions. I could imagine hearing that on my car radio on a lovely New England summer night, sure—on the one AM radio with perfect reception in the deepest depths of hell.

A host on a competing station said during the World Series that he's tired of hearing about Dave Roberts's history-altering steal in Game 4 of the 2004 ALCS. Two days after Mookie Betts—as admirable a person as he is a ballplayer—won the American League Most Valuable Player award, the same host was yelping that the Red Sox should trade him now because he could leave as a free agent after 2020. This show has been rated No. 1 in its timeslot for six consecutive years.

Some criticism in real time is always justified, of course. Price's postseason record was abysmal. The bullpen had enough aggravating moments to wonder if they were harbingers for a fatally flawed postseason performance. The Red Sox had won back to back division titles in 2016-17, only to fizzle in the divisional round each time.

But the emphasis of the negative and only the negative makes for an aggravating experience for those Red Sox fans that are level-headed rather than fretting that the bandwagon is going to careen off the highway eventually. Sports radio brainwashes too many fans into believing optimism makes you a Pollyanna. Too many fans are willing to go along with it without any critical thinking. It's not just that they're chicken littles, telling you that the sky is falling. They tell you the sky was never that great, never especially bright or blue, in the first place.

Boston Red Sox 2019

The national perception is that the assorted titles have made Boston sports fans entitled. There's some truth there, but the landscape is more complicated than any smug t-shirt slogan like they hate-us-'cause-they-ain't-us might reveal. I'll admit it: As a columnist, I still want the local teams to win. It's good for business, your stories get read by a huge audience and, if you're lucky, saved in commemoration. It's more rewarding to cover memorable accomplishments than it is devastating disappointments, and your friends who truly care about the teams are happy, at least in the immediate days afterward. The Dunkin's tastes better the morning after a championship is won, you know?

But the chronic negativity via certain media brings a warped reality, too. An exceptional victory, like the one the Red Sox authored in 2018, can feel like two victories: One over the opponent on the ballfield, and one over the culture. That culture is long ingrained. A former Boston sports anchor, the cheeky Bob Lobel, was notorious for asking, "Why can't we get players like that?" whenever an ex-Red Sox would fare well. (It was usually Jeff Bagwell.) Lobel, not so cheekily, also told us to "be careful what we wish for" when the Red Sox won in '04, as if some meaningful part of the identity of being a Boston fan was lost. Yeah, I'll take the banners over the bummers, thanks.

That deep-seated instinct for negativity adds extra degrees of difficulty for the players. It can infect and permeate a team if it is not strong in every way. It was so critical for the 2004 Red Sox to possess an indefatigable mental toughness, a goofy, fearless defiance, because a weaker-minded team could not overcome ... well, everything.

In the aftermath of the 2003 Red Sox' Game 7 loss to the Yankees in the ALCS, then-manager Grady Little acknowledged that there were players on the roster who were being crushed by the weight of history, fearful of being the next Bill Buckner. The 2018 team did not carry such a burden—it was a tight-knit and unfailingly professional clubhouse—but still, its mental toughness never wavered. They validated every belief and slaughtered every negative narrative along the way. It was incredibly impressive, and yet aggravating to that a team that won 108 regular season games had lousy narratives to slaughter at all.

I say this as someone who should have been the quintessential scarred and damaged Red Sox fan. The first year I followed baseball was 1978. I was 8. When Yaz popped up to Graig Nettles to end the one-game playoff and the Yankees commenced reveling on the Fenway lawn, I turned to my dad next to me on the couch and asked, "How do the Red Sox feel right now, dad?" It was the first dumb question in what would become a lifetime of asking dumb questions, but it elicited an answer I've never forgotten: "Well, Chad, they feel like [expletive]," he said, and then, in that eureka moment, so did I.

The 2018 season was the 40th anniversary of the Red Sox' collapse in '78, and there were no shortage of reminders of that this past season as the Red Sox built their lead over the Yankees. In a slight way, I do understand the misty watercolor nostalgia for the days of misery and disappointment. Perhaps those miserable times happened while you were watching the game with a loved one who is no longer with us or a friend who is no longer near. Perhaps it's not a longing for the time when the Red Sox would disappoint, but a longing for the time itself, when youth was still yours and days were more fulfilling. But in dwelling on days departed, so much is missed when these modern Red Sox rise to the magnitude of the moment.

During the 2018 postseason, I realized that it helps to get away from Boston to feel the spirit of true fandom. There were a thousand moments large and small through the Red Sox' championship run that felt pivotal and/or emboldening, including one that actually came in defeat: Nathan Eovaldi's six innings (and 97 pitches) of relief work on one day's rest in the 18-inning Game 3 epic.

The Red Sox tell you that defeat unified them even more, that they had tears in their eyes and steeled determination in their guts after Eovaldi's selflessness. But any claims that they were sure they were going to win the World Series at that point must be swallowed with a full shaker of salt.

After all, they trailed the Dodgers, 4-0, through six innings of Game 4. The Dodgers were nine outs from evening the series. Then, something extraordinary: Mitch Moreland connected for a three-run home run off of Pedro Baez in the seventh … and it was if a flipped switched at Chavez Ravine, as if every Dodger fan had been escorted out at that moment and replaced by a Red Sox fan. It remained Fenway West Coast for the rest of the series, through their eventual 9-6 victory in that Game 4, then the efficiently anticlimactic 5-1 victory in Game 5.

As the Red Sox rejoiced on the Dodger Stadium grass in the postgame chaos of their clinching victory, as the redeemed and beaming David Price hugged every non-reporter in sight, as Fox's David Ortiz swallowed his former teammate and understudy Mookie Betts in a bear hug, and as Alex Rodriguez tried to calculate the most authentic-seeming human emotion he could, thousands of Boston fans ringed the field, roaring deliriously, the picture of happiness, the sunshine without the clouds. The perfect picture of what being a Red Sox fan was supposed to look and feel like at the pinnacle was taken three-thousand miles away from Fenway.

In the final episode of the American version of The Office, the character Andy Bernard says, "I wish there was a way to tell you're in the good old days before you've actually left them." It's a sweet, sentimental line, but the reality is that there is a way to know—all it requires is a conscious effort and willingness to appreciate the good stuff as it is happening. I wish more Red Sox fans knew, or cared to do, this.

Sometimes it helps to get away from home to remember how fortunate we have become, to be reminded that even during the frustrating stretches that come every season that it's OK to assume things will be OK, to know that it doesn't make you soft or a Pollyanna or not a real fan because you believe in a team fully and without cynicism. The Red Sox have won four World Series titles in 15 years. Man, these are the good old days. I suppose there's some bonus satisfaction that comes in watching them silence the chronic and usually well-compensated cynics. But the greater satisfaction will come when the cynics' shrill wish-casting for disappointment stops registering at all. Maybe this will be the year. Doubt it, but crazier dreams have come true.

—Chad Finn is a columnist at the Boston Globe.

Part 2: Player Analysis

Andrew Benintendi LF

Born: 07/06/94 Age: 24 Bats: L Throws: L
Height: 5'10" Weight: 170 Origin: Round 1, 2015 Draft (#7 overall)

YEAR	TEAM	LVL	AGE	PA	R	2B	3B	HR	RBI	BB	K	SB	CS	AVG/OBP/SLG
2016	SLM	A+	21	155	30	13	7	1	32	15	9	8	2	.341/.413/.563
2016	PME	AA	21	263	40	18	5	8	44	24	30	8	7	.295/.357/.515
2016	BOS	MLB	21	118	16	11	1	2	14	10	25	1	0	.295/.359/.476
2017	BOS	MLB	22	658	84	26	1	20	90	70	112	20	5	.271/.352/.424
2018	BOS	MLB	23	661	103	41	6	16	87	71	106	21	3	.290/.366/.465
2019	BOS	MLB	24	641	88	35	4	17	67	63	111	18	4	.274/.350/.440

Breakout: 6% Improve: 48% Collapse: 13% Attrition: 9% MLB: 100%
Comparables: Mookie Betts, Rafael Palmeiro, Bruce Bochte

When a team wins 108 games—119 including the playoffs—it can be tough to come away with just one image that captures their historic greatness. But in the fifth inning of Game 2 of the World Series, Benintendi made a leaping catch in front of the Green Monster that will live on in Boston lore for many years. It was a good but not spectacular grab—in fact, it wasn't even Benintendi's most impressive catch of the postseason. But the visual was absolutely striking—an airborne Benintendi in the Air Jordan pose positioned directly in front of the iconic bright white standings that are manually entered on Fenway's great green wall. They read, in descending order: BOSTON—NEW YORK—TAMPA BAY—TORONTO—BALTIMORE, with each team's record following. That moment was the cherry on top of an outstanding sophomore season for Benintendi, who became a stronger hitter, better runner and smarter fielder in his second year. Despite some issues against same-side pitchers and a bit of a second-half swoon, Benintendi was very productive batting out of the two-spot in Boston's loaded order, and he excelled despite not turning 24 until July. He just narrowly missed out on his first All-Star selection, but if Benintendi stays on his current trajectory he'll be playing in quite a few before it's all said and done. He may never provide us with a better poster, though.

YEAR	TEAM	LVL	AGE	PA	DRC+	VORP	BABIP	BRR	FRAA	WARP
2016	SLM	A+	21	155	162	18.0	.354	-0.2	CF(30): 5.5	1.5
2016	PME	AA	21	263	136	19.4	.308	0.7	CF(53): 0.2, LF(4): 1.9	1.5
2016	BOS	MLB	21	118	92	5.0	.367	-0.6	LF(29): 0.9, CF(5): -0.2	0.2
2017	BOS	MLB	22	658	107	18.4	.301	1.4	LF(123): -0.6, CF(30): 0.0	2.5
2018	BOS	MLB	23	661	118	33.9	.328	-1.1	LF(129): 8.2, CF(24): -2.6	3.7
2019	BOS	MLB	24	641	113	29.8	.312	1.7	LF 2, CF 0	3.4

Andrew Benintendi, continued

Batted Ball Distribution

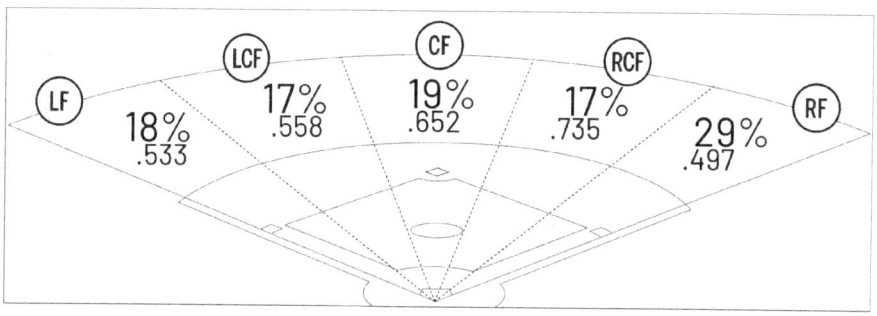

Strike Zone vs LHP

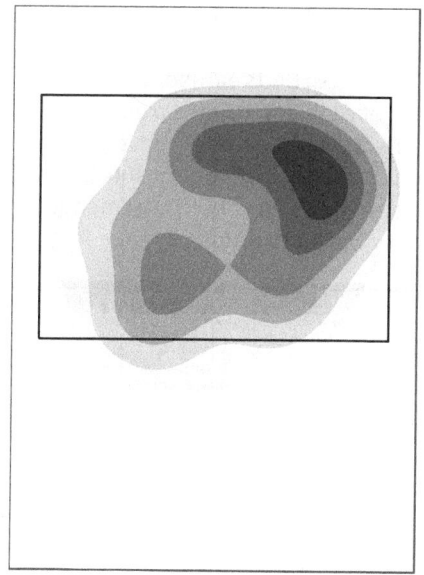

Strike Zone vs RHP

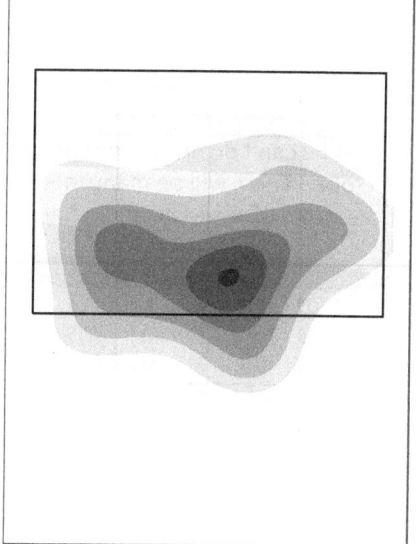

Boston Red Sox 2019

Mookie Betts RF
Born: 10/07/92 Age: 26 Bats: R Throws: R
Height: 5'9" Weight: 180 Origin: Round 5, 2011 Draft (#172 overall)

YEAR	TEAM	LVL	AGE	PA	R	2B	3B	HR	RBI	BB	K	SB	CS	AVG/OBP/SLG
2016	BOS	MLB	23	730	122	42	5	31	113	49	80	26	4	.318/.363/.534
2017	BOS	MLB	24	712	101	46	2	24	102	77	79	26	3	.264/.344/.459
2018	BOS	MLB	25	614	129	47	5	32	80	81	91	30	6	.346/.438/.640
2019	BOS	MLB	26	692	111	42	5	27	88	78	90	28	5	.303/.385/.523

Breakout: 2% Improve: 53% Collapse: 6% Attrition: 7% MLB: 99%
Comparables: Mike Greenwell, Gary Sheffield, Paul Waner

We can argue until we're all blue in the face about who the *best* player in baseball is, but it seems fairly clear-cut that Betts is the game's most well-rounded player. Per our metrics, he was the game's second-best hitter, 14th-best defender (excluding catchers) and 20th-best base runner, which is why the BBWAA named him AL MVP. He had the best batting average, scored the most runs and had the best slugging percentage in the game. He also had the third-most doubles and stole the 10th-most bases. Betts became just the second Red Sox ever to join the 30-30 club. He won his third Gold Glove and his second Silver Slugger. Since our last Annual was published, Betts earned press for feeding the homeless outside the Boston Public Library, bowled a perfect game in the World Series of Bowling and became a father. It is entirely possible there's nothing he can't do on *or* off the baseball diamond. Betts only just turned 26 in October. There will be many more accolades in his future. He is tremendous for the game of baseball, and we are all lucky we get to watch him.

YEAR	TEAM	LVL	AGE	PA	DRC+	VORP	BABIP	BRR	FRAA	WARP
2016	BOS	MLB	23	730	133	48.3	.322	8.7	RF(157): 24.8	8.0
2017	BOS	MLB	24	712	115	31.4	.268	6.2	RF(153): 23.9	5.9
2018	BOS	MLB	25	614	178	77.3	.368	3.8	RF(120): 10.7, CF(14): 0.4	8.9
2019	BOS	MLB	26	692	140	59.9	.315	3.4	RF 14, CF 0	7.2

Mookie Betts, continued

Batted Ball Distribution

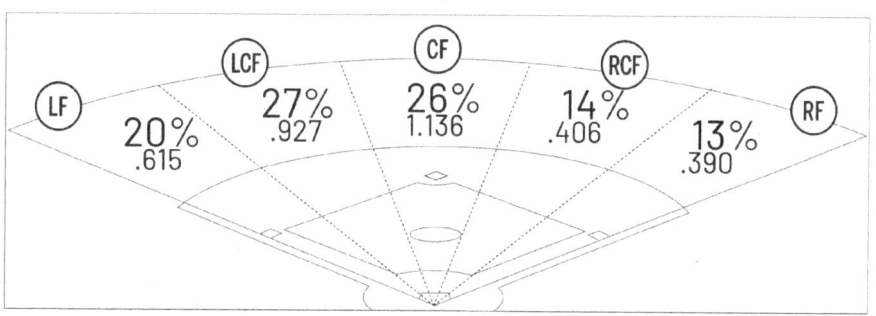

Strike Zone vs LHP

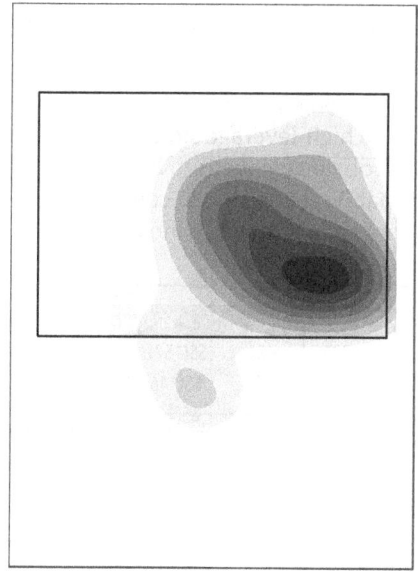

Strike Zone vs RHP

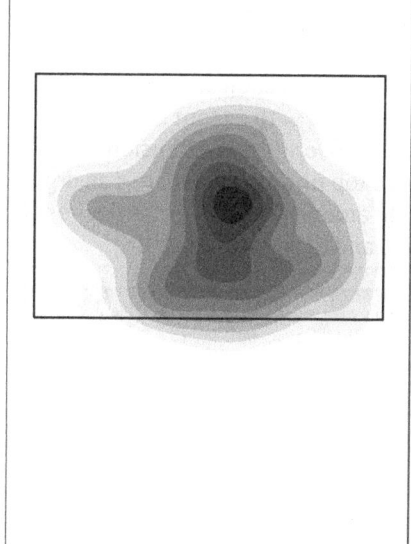

Xander Bogaerts SS

Born: 10/01/92 Age: 26 Bats: R Throws: R
Height: 6'1" Weight: 210 Origin: International Free Agent, 2009

YEAR	TEAM	LVL	AGE	PA	R	2B	3B	HR	RBI	BB	K	SB	CS	AVG/OBP/SLG
2016	BOS	MLB	23	719	115	34	1	21	89	58	123	13	4	.294/.356/.446
2017	BOS	MLB	24	635	94	32	6	10	62	56	116	15	1	.273/.343/.403
2018	BOS	MLB	25	580	72	45	3	23	103	55	102	8	2	.288/.360/.522
2019	BOS	MLB	26	597	72	30	4	16	71	59	106	11	2	.275/.352/.438

Breakout: 7% Improve: 48% Collapse: 8% Attrition: 9% MLB: 98%
Comparables: Jose Reyes, Yunel Escobar, J.J. Hardy

Patience is not a strong suit among prospect lovers, or most Red Sox fans, for that matter. Some were ready to label Bogaerts a bust after his relatively disappointing 2017 season, ignoring his youth, pedigree and the wrist injury that clearly hampered his performance. But the more enlightened knew that with better health a breakout could be just around the corner, and in 2018, at the ripe old age of 25, Bogaerts finally delivered. The Sox shortstop set career-best marks in pretty much everything other than batting average and stolen bases. Among shortstops, he finished first in doubles, second in OBP, third in slugging and fifth in both total bases and home runs. He was among Boston's best hitters, steadiest defenders and most handsome players. And he was clutch, too, with a stout .333/.390/.563 effort in high-leverage situations. When it comes to long-term extensions, Mookie Betts obviously needs to be the Red Sox's top priority. But there's an argument that Bogaerts should come next, even among a crop of potential post-2019 free agents that also includes Chris Sale and Rick Porcello.

YEAR	TEAM	LVL	AGE	PA	DRC+	VORP	BABIP	BRR	FRAA	WARP
2016	BOS	MLB	23	719	112	38.4	.335	3.3	SS(157): -11.9	3.4
2017	BOS	MLB	24	635	98	31.9	.327	5.5	SS(146): -9.2	2.4
2018	BOS	MLB	25	580	130	50.2	.317	-0.2	SS(136): 1.5	4.9
2019	BOS	MLB	26	597	113	35.7	.315	0.8	SS -8	2.5

Xander Bogaerts, continued

Batted Ball Distribution

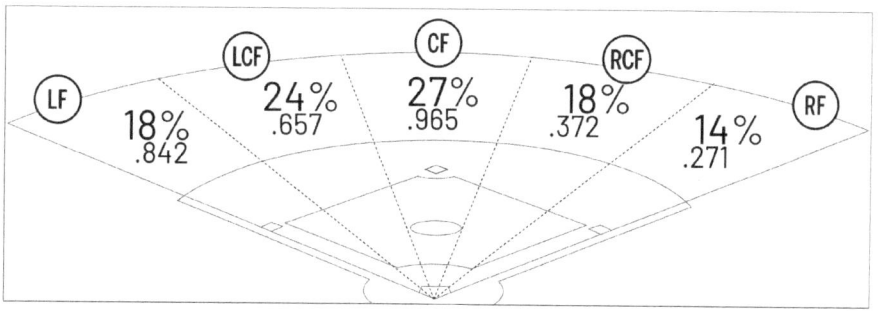

| Strike Zone vs LHP | Strike Zone vs RHP |

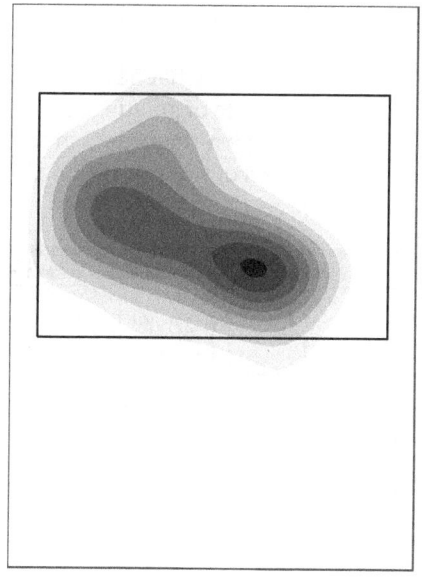 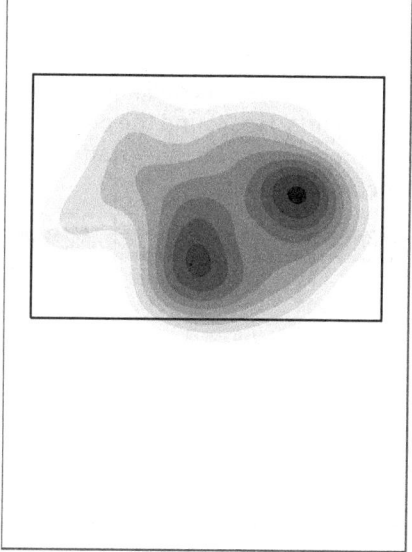

Red Sox Player Analysis - 25

Jackie Bradley CF

Born: 04/19/90 Age: 29 Bats: L Throws: R
Height: 5'10" Weight: 200 Origin: Round 1, 2011 Draft (#40 overall)

YEAR	TEAM	LVL	AGE	PA	R	2B	3B	HR	RBI	BB	K	SB	CS	AVG/OBP/SLG
2016	BOS	MLB	26	636	94	30	7	26	87	63	143	9	2	.267/.349/.486
2017	BOS	MLB	27	541	58	19	3	17	63	48	124	8	3	.245/.323/.402
2018	BOS	MLB	28	535	76	33	4	13	59	46	137	17	1	.234/.314/.403
2019	BOS	MLB	29	521	64	25	4	15	58	47	119	11	2	.251/.330/.419

Breakout: 7%   Improve: 53%   Collapse: 7%   Attrition: 14%   MLB: 99%
Comparables: Nate McLouth, Austin Jackson, Chris Young

It took Leo 27 years to win an Oscar and Henry Winkler 43 years to win an Emmy, but the real crime is that Bradley had to wait five-plus seasons for his first Gold Glove. You have to watch Bradley for only a handful of games—say a playoff series or three—to understand that he should have a few such defensive honors by now. But ALCS MVP? Well, it was harder to see that award coming. JBJ earned his Hardware by driving in nine runs against the defending champs thanks in part to a game-clinching grand slam off Roberto Osuna at Minute Maid Park in Game 3. It's fitting that Bradley earned acclaim for his bat in a series in which he recorded only three hits, as it accurately represents who and what he is at the plate: often overmatched and streaky as all hell, yet capable of greatness in small spurts. He's found the perfect role in Boston as a down-the-order hitter who props up the pitching staff with his trademark brand of smooth-looking, spectacular defense.

YEAR	TEAM	LVL	AGE	PA	DRC+	VORP	BABIP	BRR	FRAA	WARP
2016	BOS	MLB	26	636	114	31.1	.312	3.0	CF(156): 9.1	4.5
2017	BOS	MLB	27	541	96	19.3	.294	3.8	CF(132): -7.4	1.3
2018	BOS	MLB	28	535	88	15.3	.299	2.5	CF(135): 6.1, RF(15): 0.3	1.9
2019	BOS	MLB	29	521	101	23.8	.302	1.1	CF-3	1.9

Jackie Bradley, continued

Batted Ball Distribution

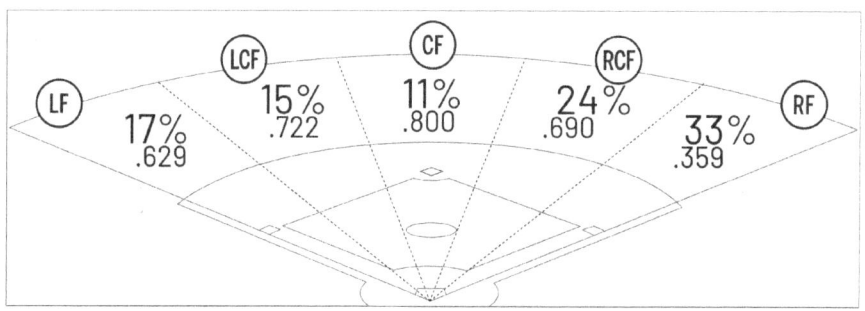

Strike Zone vs LHP   **Strike Zone vs RHP**

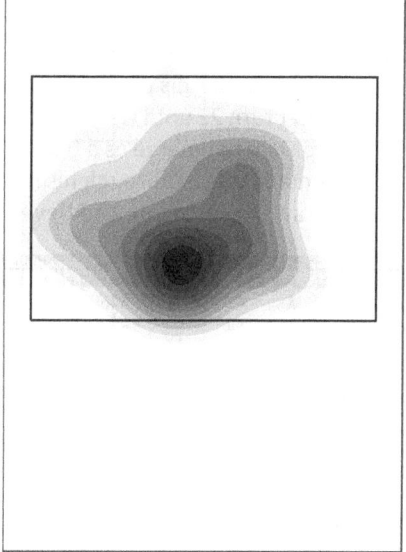

Rafael Devers 3B

Born: 10/24/96 Age: 22 Bats: L Throws: R
Height: 6'0" Weight: 237 Origin: International Free Agent, 2013

YEAR	TEAM	LVL	AGE	PA	R	2B	3B	HR	RBI	BB	K	SB	CS	AVG/OBP/SLG
2016	SLM	A+	19	546	64	32	8	11	71	40	94	18	6	.282/.335/.443
2017	PME	AA	20	320	48	19	3	18	56	31	55	0	3	.300/.369/.575
2017	PAW	AAA	20	38	6	1	0	2	4	3	8	0	0	.400/.447/.600
2017	BOS	MLB	20	240	34	14	0	10	30	18	57	3	1	.284/.338/.482
2018	BOS	MLB	21	490	59	24	0	21	66	38	121	5	2	.240/.298/.433
2019	BOS	MLB	22	477	56	24	2	18	62	40	109	4	2	.254/.320/.443

Breakout: 17% Improve: 74% Collapse: 1% Attrition: 13% MLB: 86%
Comparables: Addison Russell, Brett Lawrie, Xander Bogaerts

Boston's favorite Large Adult Son had an up-and-down first full season in the majors. Let's start with the positives: Devers finished in the top 15 among third basemen in BWARP, homers and RBI. He remains adept at crushing premium velocity, can make the occasional spectacular play at third base and had some nice postseason moments. Unfortunately, there were some real growing pains, too. Devers hit just .229/.272/.347 against southpaws, had a worse overall OBP than Pablo Sandoval and will occasionally miss first base by...oh, let's say 50 feet or so when he rushes his throws from third. It's important to remember that Devers didn't turn 22 until Game 2 of the World Series. All the raw material required for him to emerge as a true middle-of-the-order hitter and tolerable third baseman (at least through his mid-20s) remains evident. But we call raw material "raw" for a reason, and Devers needs some refinement.

YEAR	TEAM	LVL	AGE	PA	DRC+	VORP	BABIP	BRR	FRAA	WARP
2016	SLM	A+	19	546	106	25.1	.328	-1.2	3B(117): 22.2	2.8
2017	PME	AA	20	320	154	26.8	.316	-0.7	3B(64): 4.6	2.7
2017	PAW	AAA	20	38	148	5.6	.480	0.1	3B(8): -2.1	0.1
2017	BOS	MLB	20	240	106	12.0	.342	0.2	3B(56): 4.9	1.6
2018	BOS	MLB	21	490	94	13.6	.281	1.7	3B(116): 11.2	2.8
2019	BOS	MLB	22	477	99	12.3	.296	-0.5	3B 10	2.0

Rafael Devers, continued

Batted Ball Distribution

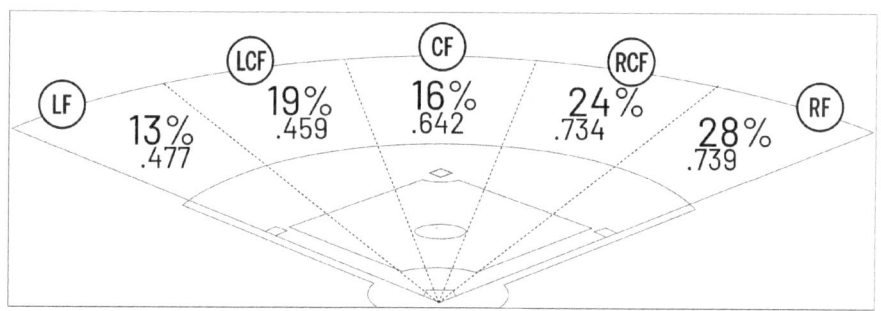

| Strike Zone vs LHP | Strike Zone vs RHP |

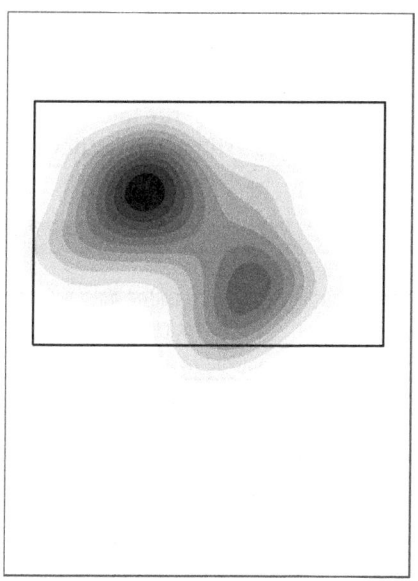 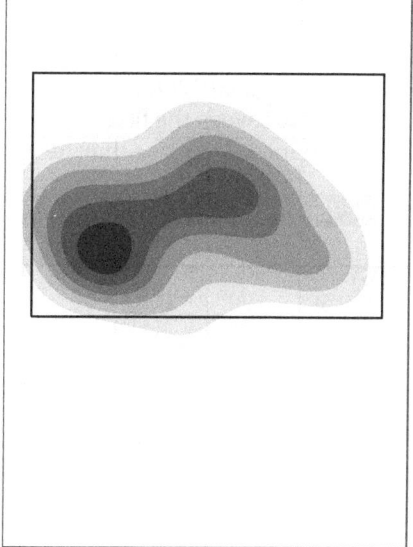

Gorkys Hernandez CF
Born: 09/07/87 Age: 31 Bats: R Throws: R
Height: 6'1" Weight: 196 Origin: International Free Agent, 2005

YEAR	TEAM	LVL	AGE	PA	R	2B	3B	HR	RBI	BB	K	SB	CS	AVG/OBP/SLG
2016	SAC	AAA	28	503	74	22	3	8	51	52	77	20	13	.302/.382/.421
2016	SFN	MLB	28	57	7	5	0	2	4	3	11	0	1	.259/.298/.463
2017	SFN	MLB	29	348	40	20	1	0	22	31	73	12	4	.255/.327/.326
2018	SFN	MLB	30	451	52	16	2	15	40	27	113	8	5	.234/.285/.391
2019	BOS	MLB	31	405	50	16	2	9	37	33	92	10	5	.239/.309/.366

Breakout: 0%   Improve: 30%   Collapse: 11%   Attrition: 22%   MLB: 71%
Comparables: Alex Presley, Chris Burke, Chris Denorfia

Ten pounds of muscle, 3.6 degrees of launch angle, 2.5 miles an hour of exit velocity and the intent to hit the ball up. Those four factors, along with a pain-free wrist, nearly tripled Hernandez's career home run total, yet the transformation hardly changed his offensive outlook overall. Gorkys the slugger was more entertaining than Gorkys the scrub, but the taters were virtually negated by a bushel of popups and a decrease in walks. While the Rockies—victims of seven Gorkys taters—never solved Hernandez, by the All-Star break, everyone else learned to steer clear of his down-and-in power alley, and he hit just .162/.220/.286 from that point on. Hernandez's true talent lies somewhere between the first and second halves, but he's still a fifth outfielder, just a more interesting one than he was before.

YEAR	TEAM	LVL	AGE	PA	DRC+	VORP	BABIP	BRR	FRAA	WARP
2016	SAC	AAA	28	503	119	35.6	.349	2.1	CF(113): -0.2	2.1
2016	SFN	MLB	28	57	93	2.2	.293	-0.1	CF(14): -0.1, RF(6): 1.0	0.2
2017	SFN	MLB	29	348	76	6.4	.331	2.3	LF(57): -5.7, CF(50): 2.4	-0.1
2018	SFN	MLB	30	451	79	7.9	.283	2.5	CF(86): -0.1, LF(37): -0.3	0.5
2019	BOS	MLB	31	405	85	8.5	.292	1.4	CF 1, LF 0	0.9

Gorkys Hernandez, continued

Batted Ball Distribution

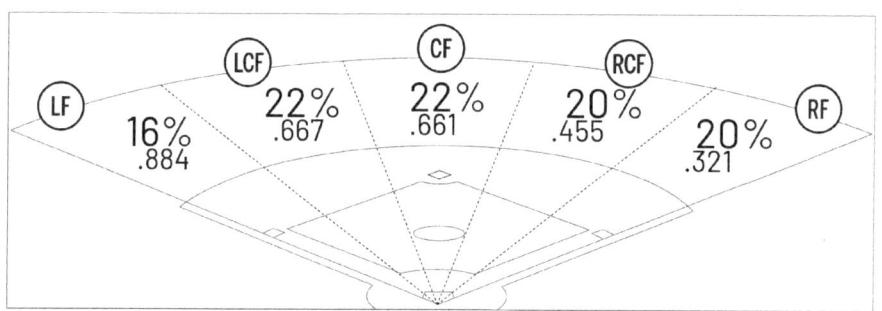

Strike Zone vs LHP **Strike Zone vs RHP**

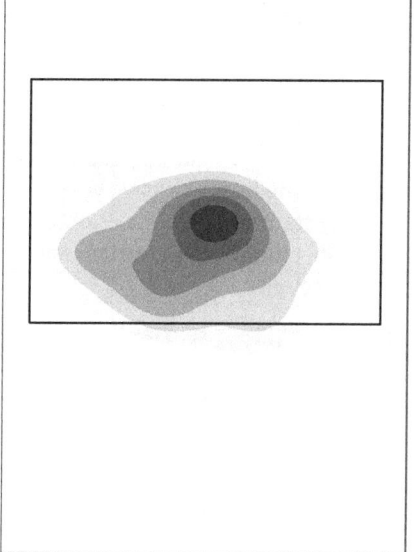

Brock Holt UT

Born: 06/11/88 Age: 31 Bats: L Throws: R
Height: 5'10" Weight: 180 Origin: Round 9, 2009 Draft (#265 overall)

YEAR	TEAM	LVL	AGE	PA	R	2B	3B	HR	RBI	BB	K	SB	CS	AVG/OBP/SLG
2016	BOS	MLB	28	324	45	16	0	7	34	27	58	4	3	.255/.322/.383
2017	PAW	AAA	29	77	9	1	0	3	9	6	14	0	0	.214/.286/.357
2017	BOS	MLB	29	164	20	6	0	0	7	19	34	2	1	.200/.305/.243
2018	BOS	MLB	30	367	41	18	2	7	46	37	73	7	7	.277/.362/.411
2019	BOS	MLB	31	335	37	15	2	7	33	30	68	5	3	.249/.326/.384

Breakout: 2% Improve: 35% Collapse: 15% Attrition: 10% MLB: 91%
Comparables: Ryan Theriot, Buddy Myer, Dutch Meyer

Major League Baseball was founded in 1903. There have been about two thousand playoff games since, which means many more thousands of players have participated in said battles. Holt became the first among them to hit for the cycle in a postseason game when he clubbed a ninth-inning homer off backup catcher Austin Romine in the Red Sox's ALDS Game 3 drubbing of their archrival Yankees. "WE ARE LIVING RENT-FREE IN THEIR HEADS," drunk New Yorkers in the bleachers screamed through tears as Holt rounded the bases. "RENT-FREE," they sobbed in unison. That moment—which also made Holt just the 26th player ever to hit for multiple cycles in a career—punctuated a nice bounceback season for Boston's favorite spark plug. Holt received his most playing time since 2015 thanks in large part to Dustin Pedroia's absence, and he responded by posting the best offensive year of his career. Would he be miscast as an everyday starter? Of course. Would Boston rather have anyone else as their super sub, clubhouse glue and resident Andrew Benintendi sidekick? Of course not. o/ forever.

YEAR	TEAM	LVL	AGE	PA	DRC+	VORP	BABIP	BRR	FRAA	WARP
2016	BOS	MLB	28	324	88	5.1	.294	1.7	LF(64): 5.4, 3B(17): 1.9	1.3
2017	PAW	AAA	29	77	82	0.6	.226	0.1	LF(7): 1.3, 3B(4): 0.1	0.1
2017	BOS	MLB	29	164	69	-3.0	.259	0.6	2B(31): 0.1, LF(10): 0.7	0.0
2018	BOS	MLB	30	367	101	13.6	.337	-1.9	2B(56): -5.3, SS(23): -2.0	0.1
2019	BOS	MLB	31	335	84	5.1	.295	-0.5	2B -3, RF 0	0.2

Brock Holt, continued

Batted Ball Distribution

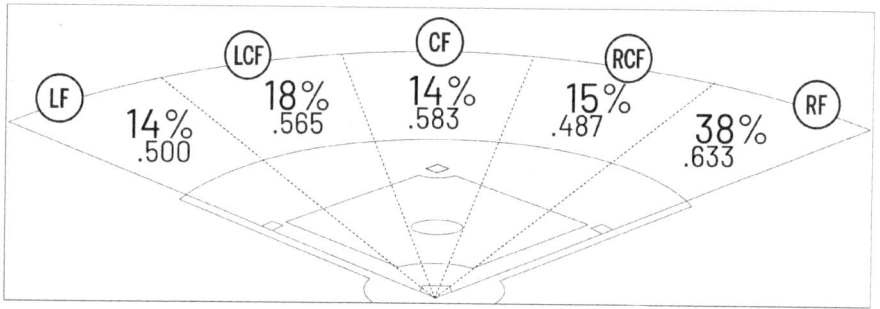

Strike Zone vs LHP

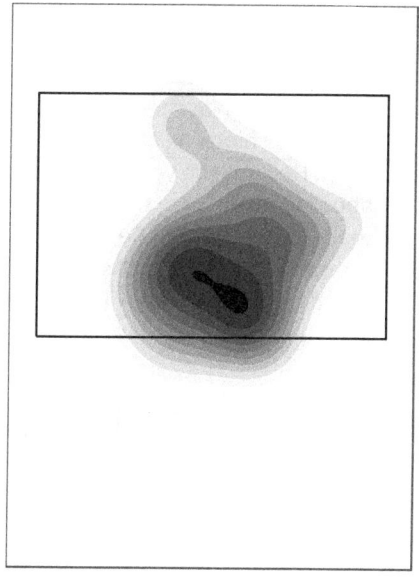

Strike Zone vs RHP

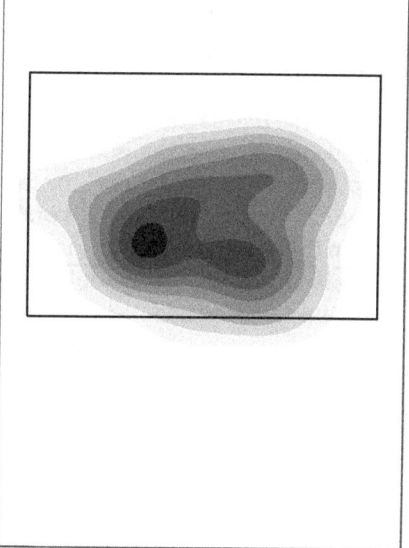

Boston Red Sox 2019

Sandy Leon C
Born: 03/13/89 Age: 30 Bats: B Throws: R
Height: 5'10" Weight: 225 Origin: International Free Agent, 2007

YEAR	TEAM	LVL	AGE	PA	R	2B	3B	HR	RBI	BB	K	SB	CS	AVG/OBP/SLG
2016	PAW	AAA	27	130	12	3	1	2	13	11	24	0	0	.243/.315/.339
2016	BOS	MLB	27	283	36	17	2	7	35	23	66	0	0	.310/.369/.476
2017	BOS	MLB	28	301	32	14	0	7	39	25	74	0	0	.225/.290/.354
2018	BOS	MLB	29	288	30	12	0	5	22	15	75	1	0	.177/.232/.279
2019	BOS	MLB	30	253	25	11	1	6	25	19	60	0	0	.232/.296/.368

Breakout: 5% Improve: 40% Collapse: 9% Attrition: 15% MLB: 84%
Comparables: Geronimo Gil, Chris Herrmann, Rob Johnson

YEAR	TEAM	P. COUNT	FRM RUNS	BLK RUNS	THRW RUNS	TOT RUNS
2016	BOS	9517	-2.1	-0.5	1.1	-1.0
2017	BOS	11373	9.7	0.4	2.0	10.7
2018	BOS	11108	11.6	0.1	0.1	11.7
2019	BOS	9493	6.7	-0.1	0.8	7.4

In "The Power of Positive Thinking," author Norman Vincent Peale asserts that the keys to happiness are to clear your mind, focus on good things you can control and forgive yourself your imperfections. Leon is a tremendous defensive catcher. In fact, it's tough to determine what the best part about his glove work is. You could argue it's his ability to steal strikes, as our Framing Runs metrics had him as the seventh-best framer in the big leagues. You could make a case for his blocking ability, as Leon allowed just 13 passed balls in 685 innings caught. Hell, maybe you'll go old school and note the way Leon's pitchers talk about him, and how they adore the way he calls games and pounces on breaking balls in the dirt. Whenever Leon looks in the mirror next, a World Series champion with a great beard will be staring back at him. He accomplished something Barry Bonds, Ted Williams and Ernie Banks never could. He also just got on base at a worse clip than Carlos Martinez.

YEAR	TEAM	LVL	AGE	PA	DRC+	VORP	BABIP	BRR	FRAA	WARP
2016	PAW	AAA	27	130	75	1.4	.286	-0.1	C(29): 6.2, 1B(1): 0.0	0.7
2016	BOS	MLB	27	283	103	20.7	.392	-1.5	C(74): -1.5	1.2
2017	BOS	MLB	28	301	74	-1.9	.280	-5.2	C(84): 10.8	1.1
2018	BOS	MLB	29	288	58	-1.3	.226	-0.7	C(87): 11.7	1.1
2019	BOS	MLB	30	253	81	4.5	.289	-0.4	C 6	1.0

Sandy Leon, continued

Batted Ball Distribution

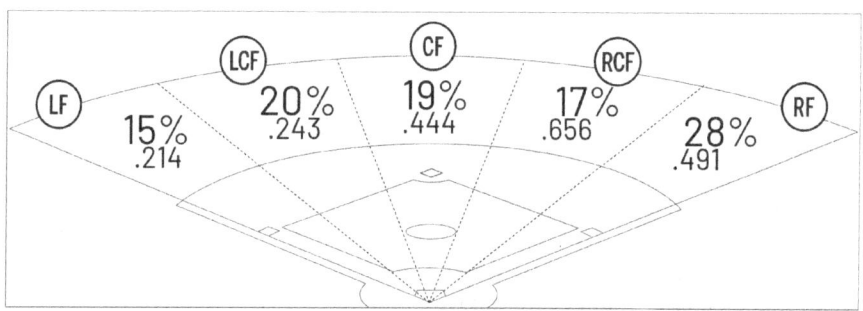

Strike Zone vs LHP   Strike Zone vs RHP

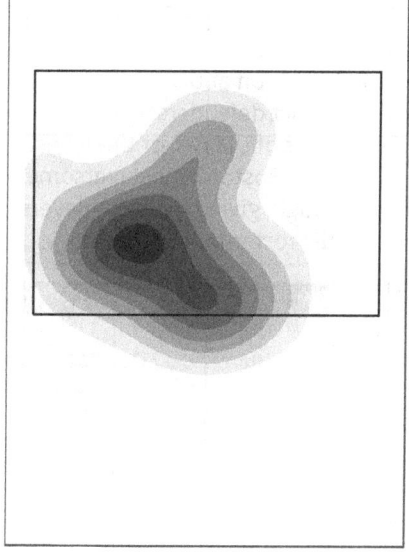

J.D. Martinez DH

Born: 08/21/87 Age: 31 Bats: R Throws: R
Height: 6'3" Weight: 220 Origin: Round 20, 2009 Draft (#611 overall)

YEAR	TEAM	LVL	AGE	PA	R	2B	3B	HR	RBI	BB	K	SB	CS	AVG/OBP/SLG
2016	DET	MLB	28	517	69	35	2	22	68	49	128	1	2	.307/.373/.535
2017	DET	MLB	29	232	38	13	2	16	39	29	54	2	0	.305/.388/.630
2017	ARI	MLB	29	257	47	13	1	29	65	24	74	2	0	.302/.366/.741
2018	BOS	MLB	30	649	111	37	2	43	130	69	146	6	1	.330/.402/.629
2019	BOS	MLB	31	650	96	37	3	36	108	74	158	5	1	.297/.379/.562

Breakout: 4% Improve: 30% Collapse: 19% Attrition: 6% MLB: 98%
Comparables: Ryan Howard, Dick Allen, Fred McGriff

Martinez did the unthinkable in his first year as a Red Sox; he hit so well that Boston shock jocks couldn't complain about his contract. Yes, Dave Dombrowski's $110-million man was worth every penny and then some in a dominant season that saw him win the 2018 AL Hank Aaron Award as the league's best hitter. Martinez finished in the top 10 in baseball among qualified batters in BWARP, homers, OBP and SLG, and first overall in total bases and RBI. He was devastatingly effective at the plate, lauded as a clubhouse leader and passable enough in the outfield to let Alex Cora occasionally give some other guys half-days off at DH. In this era of uber-athletes who are offensive threats as well as impact defenders, Martinez may never win an MVP award. But he's arguably one of the two or three best pure hitters in the game at present, and he's perhaps Boston's most fearsome right-handed hitter since Manny Ramirez. Oddly enough, giving the best players in the game a lot of money can still be a pretty solid roster-building strategy.

YEAR	TEAM	LVL	AGE	PA	DRC+	VORP	BABIP	BRR	FRAA	WARP
2016	DET	MLB	28	517	128	24.0	.378	-7.3	RF(118): -11.2	1.0
2017	DET	MLB	29	232	162	17.9	.338	-1.5	RF(53): -6.3	1.5
2017	ARI	MLB	29	257	158	26.7	.315	-2.4	RF(60): -3.9	1.8
2018	BOS	MLB	30	649	167	58.1	.375	-3.9	LF(32): -0.9, RF(25): 2.4	6.3
2019	BOS	MLB	31	650	147	44.8	.350	-0.6	LF 0, RF 0	5.1

J.D. Martinez, continued

Batted Ball Distribution

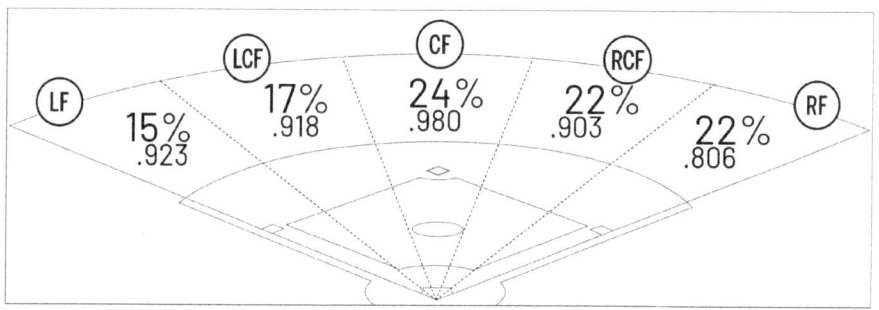

Strike Zone vs LHP

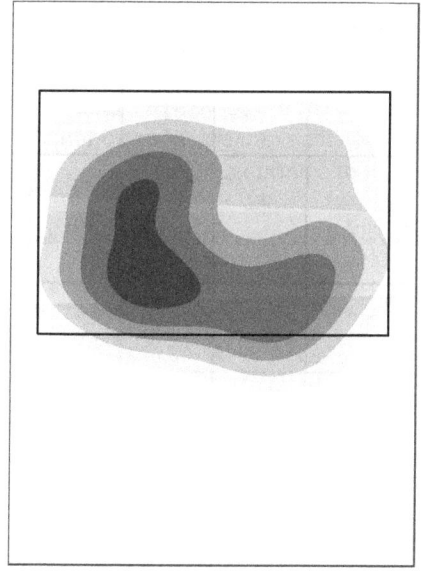

Strike Zone vs RHP

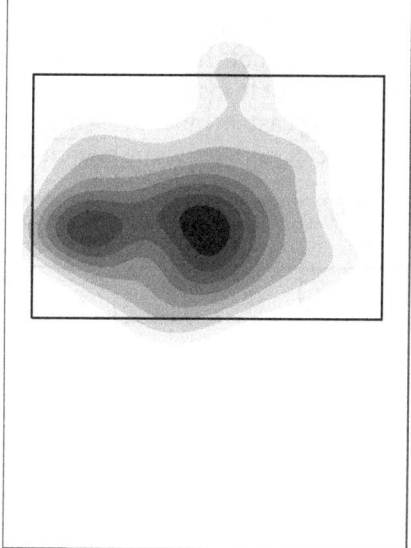

Mitch Moreland 1B

Born: 09/06/85   Age: 33   Bats: L   Throws: L
Height: 6'2"   Weight: 230   Origin: Round 17, 2007 Draft (#530 overall)

YEAR	TEAM	LVL	AGE	PA	R	2B	3B	HR	RBI	BB	K	SB	CS	AVG/OBP/SLG
2016	TEX	MLB	30	503	49	21	0	22	60	35	118	1	0	.233/.298/.422
2017	BOS	MLB	31	576	73	34	0	22	79	57	120	0	1	.246/.326/.443
2018	BOS	MLB	32	459	57	23	4	15	68	50	102	2	0	.245/.325/.433
2019	BOS	MLB	33	395	44	21	2	12	48	36	84	1	0	.249/.324/.422

Breakout: 0%   Improve: 25%   Collapse: 17%   Attrition: 19%   MLB: 92%
Comparables: Eddie Robinson, Jim Spencer, Don Mincher

You know you've reached the final Galaxy Brain level of kvetching about sports contracts when Moreland's two-year, $13 million deal gets raked over the coals. A small sample of players who made more than Moreland last season: Drew Smyly, Michael Dunn, Brett Cecil, Michael Pineda and Joe Smith. Two of those guys didn't even pitch! But for the low, low price of $6.5 million, the Sox got a guy who hit .246/.331/.450 with 13 homers off righties, mashed one of the biggest homers of the championship run and continued to play a very solid first base. Moreland is a second-division starter/platoon option through and through, but *not* signing a guy like that for your $230 million-plus payroll is like opting not to insure your Mercedes-Benz. He should serve as a capable supporting cast member again in 2019, but even if he tanks all of a sudden, the Red Sox can cut him for the payroll equivalent of a parking ticket.

YEAR	TEAM	LVL	AGE	PA	DRC+	VORP	BABIP	BRR	FRAA	WARP
2016	TEX	MLB	30	503	95	-6.2	.266	-3.0	1B(139): 3.8	0.4
2017	BOS	MLB	31	576	103	3.5	.278	-2.7	1B(138): 5.7, P(1): 0.0	1.3
2018	BOS	MLB	32	459	103	3.8	.288	-2.5	1B(116): 2.4	0.8
2019	BOS	MLB	33	395	102	6.9	.292	-0.5	1B 1	1.0

Mitch Moreland, continued

Batted Ball Distribution

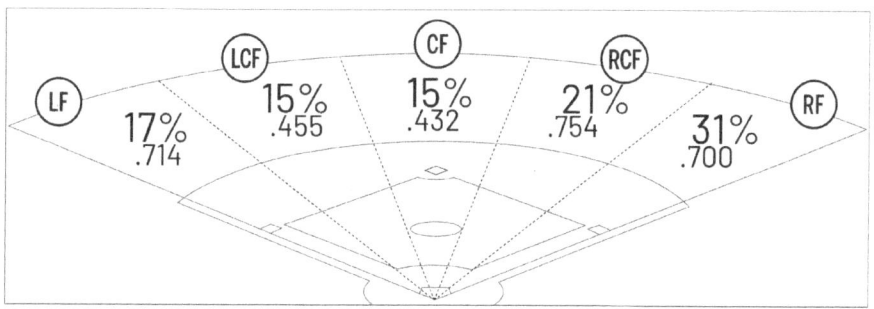

Strike Zone vs LHP

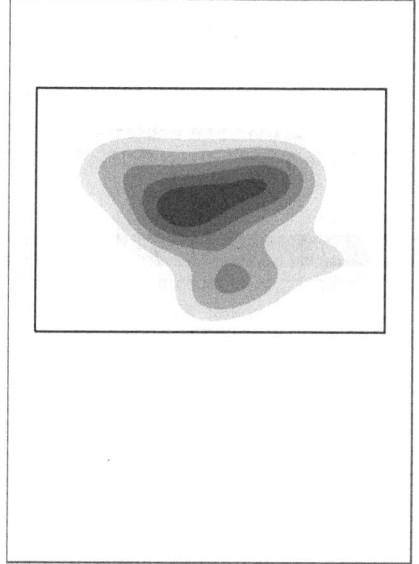

Strike Zone vs RHP

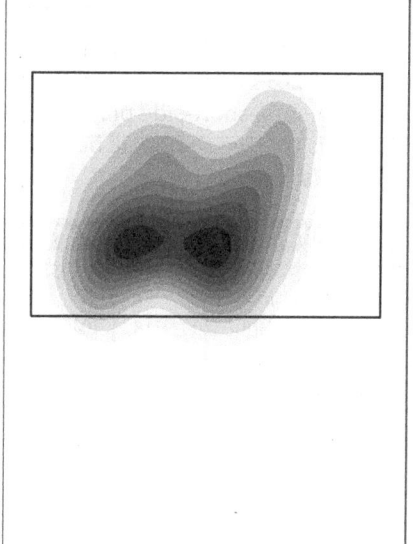

Eduardo Nunez INF

Born: 06/15/87 Age: 32 Bats: R Throws: R
Height: 6'0" Weight: 195 Origin: International Free Agent, 2004

YEAR	TEAM	LVL	AGE	PA	R	2B	3B	HR	RBI	BB	K	SB	CS	AVG/OBP/SLG
2016	MIN	MLB	29	396	49	15	1	12	47	15	58	27	6	.296/.325/.439
2016	SFN	MLB	29	199	24	9	3	4	20	14	30	13	4	.269/.327/.418
2017	SFN	MLB	30	318	37	21	0	4	31	12	29	18	5	.308/.334/.417
2017	BOS	MLB	30	173	23	12	0	8	27	6	25	6	2	.321/.353/.539
2018	BOS	MLB	31	502	56	23	3	10	44	16	69	7	2	.265/.289/.388
2019	BOS	MLB	32	299	36	14	2	7	30	17	45	11	3	.271/.315/.412

Breakout: 1% Improve: 24% Collapse: 15% Attrition: 7% MLB: 94%
Comparables: Omar Infante, Freddy Sanchez, Ronnie Belliard

Did Nunez have a good year or a bad year? On one hand, he was hurt constantly, his glove was a tire fire at second base and he basically stopped running altogether. He also posted his worst offensive season since 2014. By the time the World Series rolled around, Nunez was a collection of interconnected injured limbs, flailing about the diamond en route to spectacular plays, terrible plays and little in between. On the other hand, Nunez just won a ring! He also hit a big pinch-hit homer in Game 1 of the World Series and opted into a $5 million contact for 2019 to play for the defending champs. It's unclear as to exactly what his role will be—short-side platoon third baseman seems most likely—but what *is* clear is that we should all be so lucky as to have our rough stretches look like Nunie's.

YEAR	TEAM	LVL	AGE	PA	DRC+	VORP	BABIP	BRR	FRAA	WARP
2016	MIN	MLB	29	396	101	20.7	.320	4.8	SS(51): -1.8, 3B(33): -0.1	1.8
2016	SFN	MLB	29	199	98	10.1	.302	1.4	3B(48): 3.8, SS(4): -0.3	1.2
2017	SFN	MLB	30	318	104	18.8	.328	4.4	3B(49): -0.1, LF(19): 2.3	1.8
2017	BOS	MLB	30	173	105	12.0	.341	-1.2	2B(26): -0.8, SS(5): 0.0	0.5
2018	BOS	MLB	31	502	84	-1.0	.290	-2.6	2B(74): -2.0, 3B(45): 1.2	0.2
2019	BOS	MLB	32	299	90	6.0	.299	1.1	3B 0, 2B -1	0.5

Eduardo Nunez, continued

Batted Ball Distribution

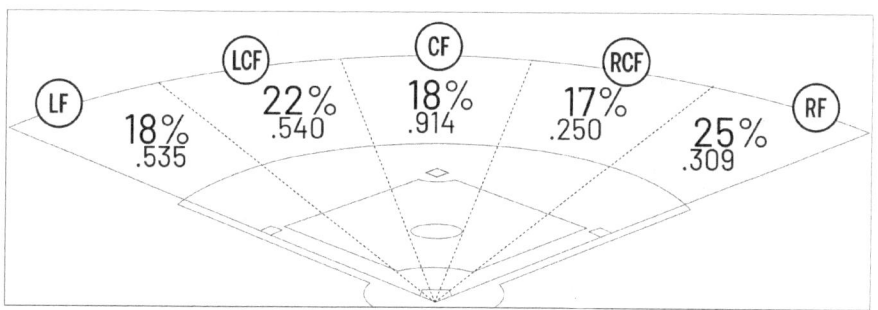

Strike Zone vs LHP   Strike Zone vs RHP

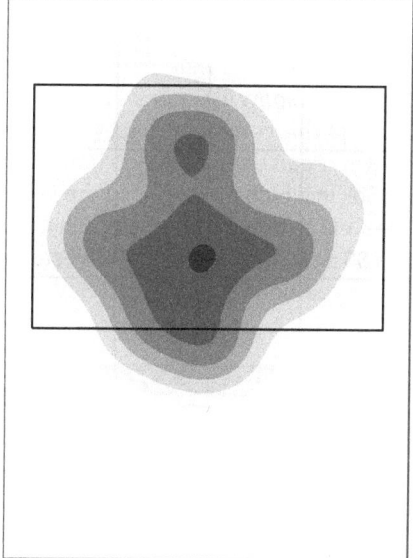

Boston Red Sox 2019

Steve Pearce 1B
Born: 04/13/83   Age: 36   Bats: R   Throws: R
Height: 5'11"   Weight: 200   Origin: Round 8, 2005 Draft (#241 overall)

YEAR	TEAM	LVL	AGE	PA	R	2B	3B	HR	RBI	BB	K	SB	CS	AVG/OBP/SLG
2016	TBA	MLB	33	232	26	11	1	10	29	26	40	0	3	.309/.388/.520
2016	BAL	MLB	33	70	9	2	0	3	6	8	14	0	0	.217/.329/.400
2017	TOR	MLB	34	348	38	17	1	13	37	27	68	0	0	.252/.319/.438
2018	TOR	MLB	35	86	16	6	0	4	16	7	14	0	0	.291/.349/.519
2018	BOS	MLB	35	165	19	8	1	7	26	22	27	0	0	.279/.394/.507
2019	BOS	MLB	36	401	45	19	2	12	49	39	79	1	1	.259/.339/.425

Breakout: 0%   Improve: 21%   Collapse: 20%   Attrition: 11%   MLB: 87%
Comparables: Rafael Palmeiro, Hideki Matsui, Travis Hafner

Between the Red Sox and Dodgers, there were 50 total players who staked claim to World Series roster spots. There were probably 43 or 44 guys more likely to win Series MVP than Pearce. But when it comes to the weird, the unpredictable and the feel-good, baseball remains undefeated. Acquired from the Blue Jays in July for the low, low cost of historical footnote/middling infield prospect Santiago Espinal, Pearce went 4-for-12 and drove in eight runs in the Fall Classic. Three of those hits were homers, and two of them came off Kenley Jansen and Clayton Kershaw in Games 4 and 5, respectively. Joe Buck would like to interrupt this comment to let you know that Pearce grew up a Red Sox fan. Anyway, Pearce's postseason heroics capped a successful second-half stint with the Sox in which he served as the perfect right-handed complement to Mitch Moreland to add another lefty-killing presence to Boston's deep lineup. He'll turn 36 next April, but that didn't stop the Sox from giving him a one-year, $6.5 million reunion tour contract. Hey, can you really put a price on The Clutch Gene?

YEAR	TEAM	LVL	AGE	PA	DRC+	VORP	BABIP	BRR	FRAA	WARP
2016	TBA	MLB	33	232	126	18.3	.342	0.0	1B(30): 1.7, 2B(14): 0.4	1.4
2016	BAL	MLB	33	70	128	3.3	.233	1.5	1B(10): -0.3, LF(7): -0.1	0.5
2017	TOR	MLB	34	348	100	7.4	.281	0.3	LF(85): 3.3, 1B(10): -0.4	1.2
2018	TOR	MLB	35	86	130	5.2	.311	0.7	LF(9): -1.4, 1B(3): 0.4	0.5
2018	BOS	MLB	35	165	133	10.8	.298	-1.4	1B(31): -1.0, RF(2): -0.1	0.7
2019	BOS	MLB	36	401	106	11.4	.301	-0.9	1B 0	1.0

Steve Pearce, continued

Batted Ball Distribution

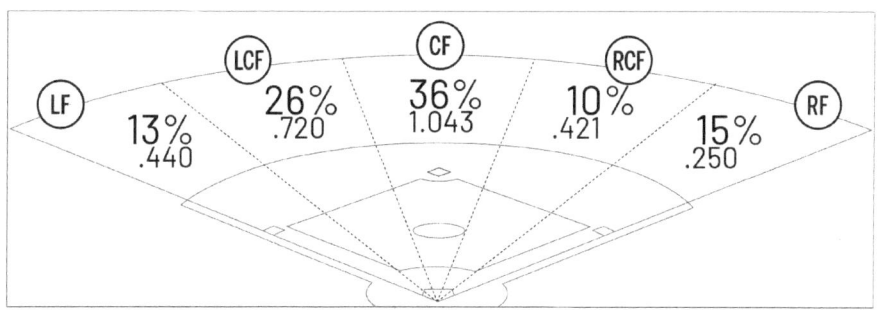

Strike Zone vs LHP

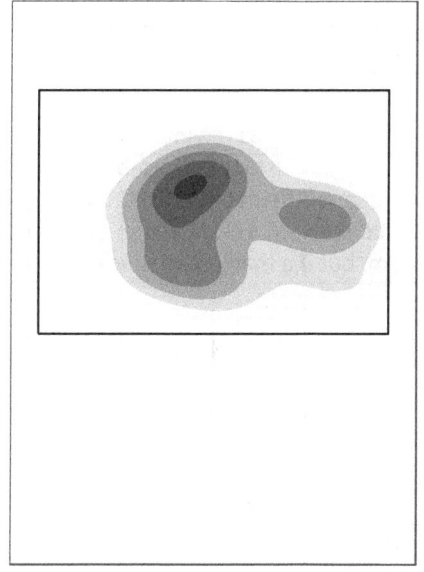

Strike Zone vs RHP

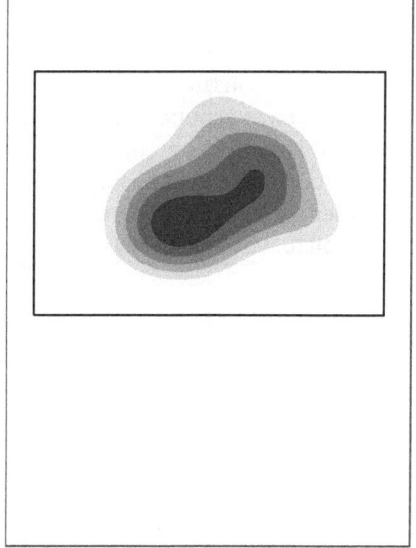

Blake Swihart   C

Born: 04/03/92   Age: 27   Bats: B   Throws: R
Height: 6'1"   Weight: 200   Origin: Round 1, 2011 Draft (#26 overall)

YEAR	TEAM	LVL	AGE	PA	R	2B	3B	HR	RBI	BB	K	SB	CS	AVG/OBP/SLG
2016	PAW	AAA	24	122	13	4	0	1	8	17	17	2	1	.243/.344/.311
2016	BOS	MLB	24	74	9	0	3	0	5	11	17	0	1	.258/.365/.355
2017	PAW	AAA	25	212	22	6	1	4	23	13	54	1	0	.190/.246/.292
2017	BOS	MLB	25	7	1	0	0	0	0	2	3	0	0	.200/.429/.200
2018	BOS	MLB	26	207	28	10	0	3	18	15	57	6	1	.229/.285/.328
2019	BOS	MLB	27	162	16	6	1	4	15	12	41	2	1	.209/.272/.345

Breakout: 10%   Improve: 47%   Collapse: 10%   Attrition: 27%   MLB: 90%
Comparables: Martin Maldonado, Christian Vazquez, James McCann

Swihart was, to put it kindly, the vestigial organ of the 2018 Red Sox. Despite nominally appearing in just over half of the team's games, he received only 12 more plate appearances than Hanley Ramirez, who was released in May. He saw only 50 more innings in the field than Ian Kinsler, who was acquired as a part-time player on July 31. Swihart had one more post-season at-bat than Nate Eovaldi. He was the team's third-best catcher, fourth-best first baseman and sixth-best outfielder. He'll be 27 shortly after Opening Day 2019. There is no prospect shine left here. Men don't cut their nipples off just because they don't need them, but if a man could save only 25 body parts ...

YEAR	TEAM	P. COUNT	FRM RUNS	BLK RUNS	THRW RUNS	TOT RUNS
2016	BOS	908	-0.4	-0.7	0.0	-1.1
2017	BOS	187	0.1	-0.5	0.0	-0.4
2017	PAW	6033	6.0	-0.5	0.2	5.4
2018	BOS	2800	0.7	0.7	0.0	1.4
2019	BOS	2456	0.5	-0.2	0.0	0.3

YEAR	TEAM	LVL	AGE	PA	DRC+	VORP	BABIP	BRR	FRAA	WARP
2016	PAW	AAA	24	122	97	2.1	.276	-0.2	C(15): 0.3, LF(11): 1.4	0.4
2016	BOS	MLB	24	74	82	0.5	.348	-0.6	LF(13): 1.0, C(6): -1.2	0.0
2017	PAW	AAA	25	212	44	-7.7	.239	-1.7	C(43): 5.0, 1B(3): 0.2	-0.3
2017	BOS	MLB	25	7	76	-0.1	.500	-0.2	C(4): -0.4	-0.1
2018	BOS	MLB	26	207	72	-2.9	.311	0.7	C(28): 1.1, RF(14): -1.9	-0.1
2019	BOS	MLB	27	162	63	-1.7	.256	0.1	C 0, LF 1	-0.2

Blake Swihart, continued

Batted Ball Distribution

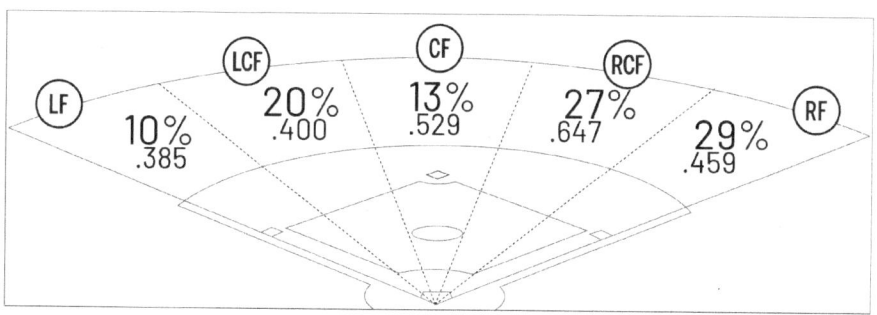

Strike Zone vs LHP

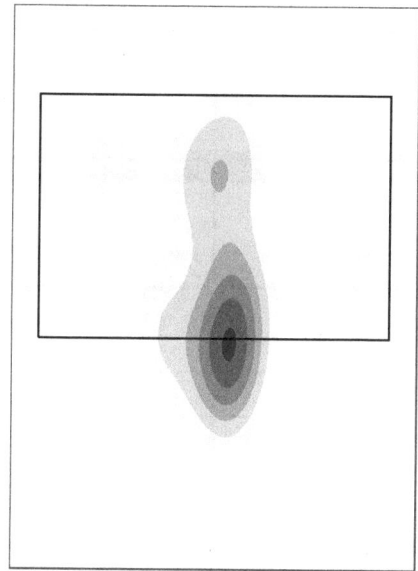

Strike Zone vs RHP

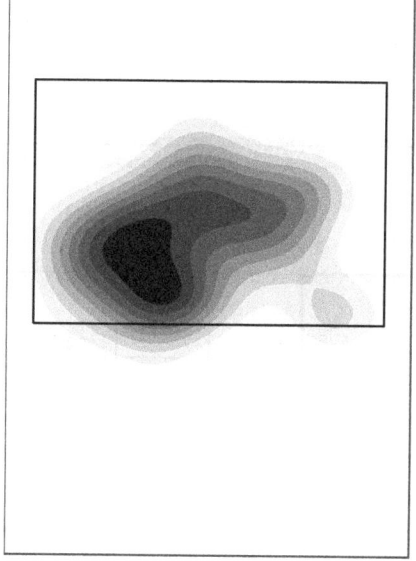

Sam Travis 1B

Born: 08/27/93 Age: 25 Bats: R Throws: R
Height: 6'0" Weight: 205 Origin: Round 2, 2014 Draft (#67 overall)

YEAR	TEAM	LVL	AGE	PA	R	2B	3B	HR	RBI	BB	K	SB	CS	AVG/OBP/SLG
2016	PAW	AAA	22	190	26	10	0	6	29	15	40	1	0	.272/.332/.434
2017	PAW	AAA	23	342	40	14	0	6	24	37	57	6	2	.270/.351/.375
2017	BOS	MLB	23	83	13	6	0	0	1	6	23	1	0	.263/.325/.342
2018	PAW	AAA	24	398	35	13	0	8	43	29	89	1	2	.258/.317/.360
2018	BOS	MLB	24	38	5	3	0	1	7	2	10	0	0	.222/.263/.389
2019	BOS	MLB	25	34	3	1	0	1	4	2	8	0	0	.226/.273/.355

Breakout: 6% Improve: 17% Collapse: 2% Attrition: 17% MLB: 28%
Comparables: Chris Marrero, Scott Thorman, Gaby Sanchez

Even die-hard Red Sox fans probably didn't hear much about Travis last year, and that's because there's relatively little to say. Boston's second-round pick from 2014 still can't stay healthy and still doesn't hit for power, and now his hit tool isn't impressing in Triple-A either. You always had to squint to look at Travis and see a starting first baseman, but it seemed like he'd at least be able to carve out a role as a platoon guy or bench bat. Maybe he still can but he's trending about as well as Papa John's stock right now. He probably makes better pizza at least.

YEAR	TEAM	LVL	AGE	PA	DRC+	VORP	BABIP	BRR	FRAA	WARP
2016	PAW	AAA	22	190	120	7.8	.320	1.4	1B(34): 2.1	0.7
2017	PAW	AAA	23	342	116	0.3	.315	-3.5	1B(58): -0.1	0.1
2017	BOS	MLB	23	83	68	-3.8	.377	-1.0	1B(21): 0.2	-0.3
2018	PAW	AAA	24	398	95	9.1	.317	1.3	1B(45): 0.5, LF(36): -2.7	-0.2
2018	BOS	MLB	24	38	80	-0.4	.280	0.0	LF(6): 0.0, 1B(3): -0.1	0.0
2019	BOS	MLB	25	34	63	-0.9	.294	-0.1	1B 0	-0.1

Sam Travis, continued

Batted Ball Distribution

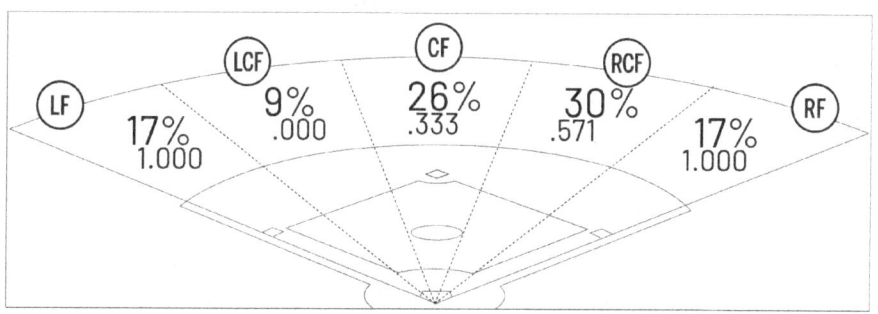

Strike Zone vs LHP

Strike Zone vs RHP

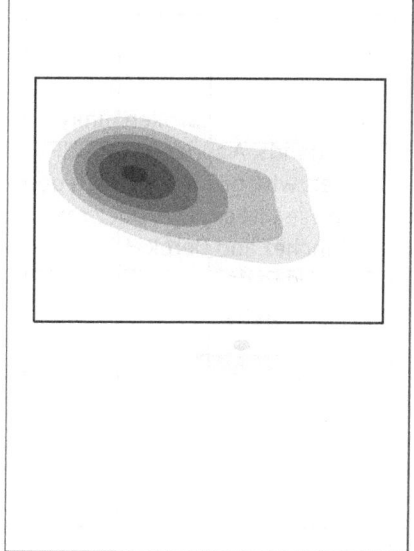

Christian Vazquez C

Born: 08/21/90   Age: 28   Bats: R   Throws: R
Height: 5'9"   Weight: 195   Origin: Round 9, 2008 Draft (#292 overall)

YEAR	TEAM	LVL	AGE	PA	R	2B	3B	HR	RBI	BB	K	SB	CS	AVG/OBP/SLG
2016	PAW	AAA	25	171	19	9	0	2	16	15	31	2	0	.270/.345/.368
2016	BOS	MLB	25	184	21	9	1	1	12	10	39	0	0	.227/.277/.308
2017	BOS	MLB	26	345	43	18	2	5	32	17	64	7	2	.290/.330/.404
2018	BOS	MLB	27	269	24	10	0	3	16	13	41	4	1	.207/.257/.283
2019	BOS	MLB	28	317	34	15	1	6	31	23	59	4	1	.253/.315/.375

Breakout: 10%   Improve: 53%   Collapse: 7%   Attrition: 18%   MLB: 94%
Comparables: Tony Cruz, Jordan Pacheco, Josh Thole

The Red Sox led the majors in a whole bunch of offensive categories last season, and the fact that they did so despite giving Vazquez north of 250 plate appearances is absolutely stunning. Vazquez placed 73rd *among catchers* in DRC+ last season.

YEAR	TEAM	P. COUNT	FRM RUNS	BLK RUNS	THRW RUNS	TOT RUNS
2016	BOS	7176	8.6	-0.8	-0.1	7.5
2017	BOS	13558	15.5	1.0	2.4	19.6
2018	BOS	10330	9.0	0.1	0.1	9.0
2019	BOS	12519	10.7	0.0	0.7	11.4

If that stat was a tweet, it'd get ratio-ed but still end up with a better line than Vazquez. His best offensive stint came between July 8 and September 1 when he was on the DL with a broken pinky. Ozzy Osbourne is more trustworthy with a bat in his hands. A super-low BABIP is partly to blame, but not as much to blame as Vazquez, who hits a few clutch bombs and almost literally nothing else every year. The eye test says Vazquez remains a wonderful defender, but Ivan Nova, Anibal Sanchez and Derek Holland were better at the plate last season. Vazquez doesn't need to do much offensively to justify his roster spot, but he needs to do more than nothing.

YEAR	TEAM	LVL	AGE	PA	DRC+	VORP	BABIP	BRR	FRAA	WARP
2016	PAW	AAA	25	171	121	9.4	.325	0.3	C(41): 5.2	1.5
2016	BOS	MLB	25	184	64	-4.0	.288	-0.7	C(56): 7.8	0.8
2017	BOS	MLB	26	345	93	7.0	.348	-3.3	C(95): 16.4, 3B(2): 0.0	2.7
2018	BOS	MLB	27	269	71	-5.4	.237	-0.4	C(75): 8.3, 3B(2): 0.0	1.2
2019	BOS	MLB	28	317	84	7.5	.295	0.0	C 9	1.7

Christian Vazquez, continued

Batted Ball Distribution

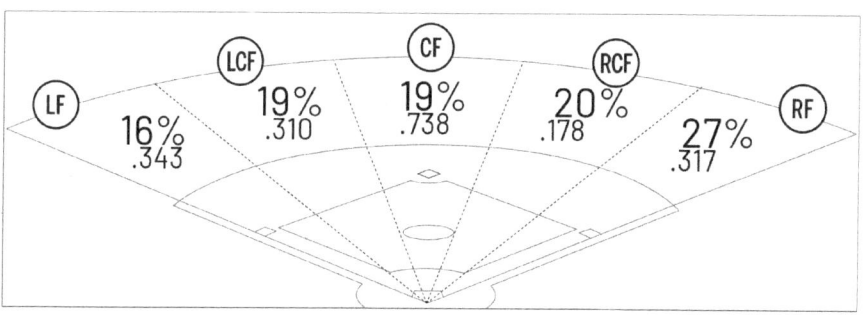

Strike Zone vs LHP

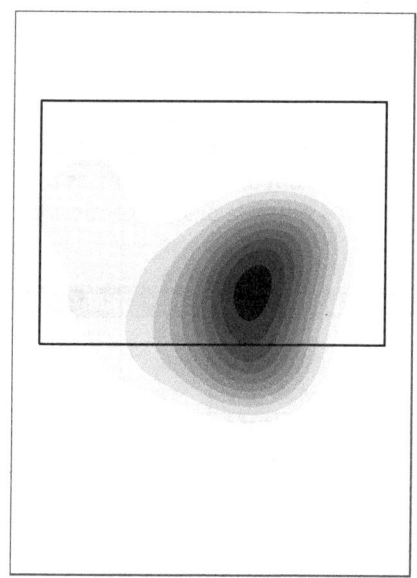

Strike Zone vs RHP

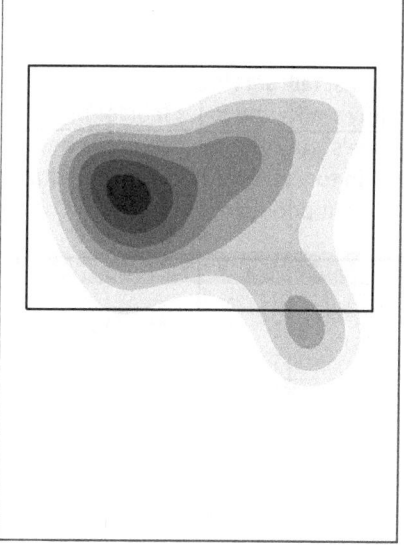

Matt Barnes RHP

Born: 06/17/90 Age: 29 Bats: R Throws: R
Height: 6'4" Weight: 210 Origin: Round 1, 2011 Draft (#19 overall)

YEAR	TEAM	LVL	AGE	W	L	SV	G	GS	IP	H	HR	BB/9	K/9	K	GB%	BABIP
2016	BOS	MLB	26	4	3	1	62	0	66^2	62	6	4.2	9.6	71	46%	.318
2017	BOS	MLB	27	7	3	1	70	0	69^2	57	7	3.6	10.7	83	50%	.298
2018	BOS	MLB	28	6	4	0	62	0	61^2	47	5	4.5	14.0	96	53%	.321
2019	BOS	MLB	29	3	3	24	53	0	55	44	4	4.1	11.6	72	48%	.301

Breakout: 28% Improve: 61% Collapse: 17% Attrition: 21% MLB: 96%
Comparables: Zach Putnam, Nick Masset, Brett Cecil

We might owe Barnes an apology. Barnes' last few Annual comments have judged his performance through the lens of a former first-round pick, and with that context he may still seem disappointing. But Barnes was drafted in 2011 and we should be over it by now. While the visions of a No. 3 starter that once danced in our heads may never come to be, we can appreciate Barnes for what he *has* become: a damn fine reliever. Barnes had easily the best season of his career in 2018, posting a slew of personal-best stats and whiffing well more than a third of the batters he faced. Whereas Barnes faded badly enough down the stretch in 2017 to get left off the postseason roster, he was a force for the Red Sox last fall, serving as Alex Cora's most reliable setup option. He still issues too many walks and loses feel for his curveball too often to be considered one of the game's truly elite relievers. But he no longer seems out of place serving as the Robin to a closer's Batman, and that makes him a valuable piece regardless of his draft pedigree.

YEAR	TEAM	LVL	AGE	WHIP	ERA	DRA	WARP	MPH	FB%	WHF	CSP
2016	BOS	MLB	26	1.39	4.05	4.68	0.2	99.1	65.4	11.9	43.6
2017	BOS	MLB	27	1.22	3.88	3.30	1.5	96.8	55	13.2	42.7
2018	BOS	MLB	28	1.26	3.65	2.21	1.9	98.4	54.8	15	42.7
2019	BOS	MLB	29	1.25	2.49	3.04	1.4	97.3	57.6	13.6	42.9

Matt Barnes, continued

Pitch Shape vs LHH

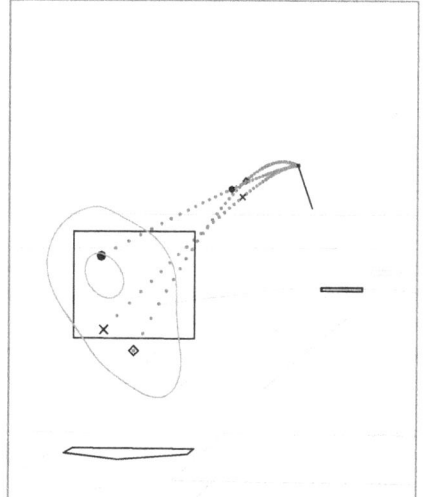

Pitch Shape vs RHH

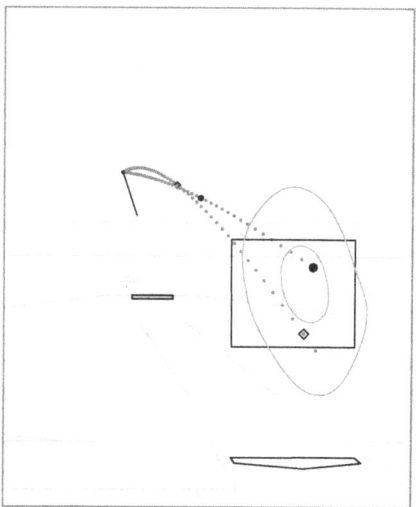

Type	Frequency	Velocity	H Movement	V Movement
● Fastball	54.8%	97.1 [115]	-7.9 [94]	-11.1 [115]
☐ Sinker				
+ Cutter				
▲ Changeup				
✕ Splitter	4.6%	89.8 [122]	-10.8 [90]	-26.5 [113]
▽ Slider	1.4%	84.9 [102]	3.2 [93]	-44.9 [65]
◇ Curveball	39.2%	84.9 [124]	3.4 [81]	-44.3 [108]
⊕ Slow Curveball				
✳ Knuckleball				
▼ Screwball				

Ryan Brasier   RHP

Born: 08/26/87   Age: 31   Bats: R   Throws: R
Height: 6'0"   Weight: 225   Origin: Round 6, 2007 Draft (#208 overall)

YEAR	TEAM	LVL	AGE	W	L	SV	G	GS	IP	H	HR	BB/9	K/9	K	GB%	BABIP
2016	NAS	AAA	28	5	3	1	46	0	60^2	50	6	2.8	10.4	70	46%	.293
2018	PAW	AAA	30	2	5	13	34	0	40^1	29	1	1.8	8.9	40	43%	.277
2018	BOS	MLB	30	2	0	0	34	0	33^2	19	2	1.9	7.8	29	43%	.198
2019	BOS	MLB	31	2	3	14	48	0	50	48	7	3.4	8.6	48	43%	.290

Breakout: 12%   Improve: 27%   Collapse: 22%   Attrition: 20%   MLB: 55%
Comparables: Dane De La Rosa, Adam Liberatore, Miguel Socolovich

Every good team gets key performances from unexpected sources, but for the 2018 Red Sox no contributor was perhaps as unexpected as Brasier. The former Weatherford College Coyote went 49 months in between MLB appearances thanks in part to Tommy John surgery. The former Angel and Athletic spent 2017 in Japan pitching for the Hiroshima Carp, where he impressed enough that the Sox offered him a minor-league contract last offseason. After dominating Triple-A for three-plus months, Brasier got the call to the big leagues in early July and never looked back. He dealt down the stretch, touching 99 and missing bats with a nasty slider, ultimately sliding right into a shockingly high-leverage role in October. He was brilliant, allowing just one run across three series of heavy usage, but he really sealed the deal with Red Sox Nation when he barked at Gary Sanchez to "get in the f***ing box" during Game 2 of the ALDS, then promptly struck his ass out. Given Brasier's strange path and general reliever volatility, there's no real way to know who and what Brasier will be moving forward. But even if 2018 is the best we'll ever see from him, it makes for a hell of a comeback story.

YEAR	TEAM	LVL	AGE	WHIP	ERA	DRA	WARP	MPH	FB%	WHF	CSP
2016	NAS	AAA	28	1.14	3.56	2.71	1.6				
2018	PAW	AAA	30	0.92	1.34	3.33	0.8				
2018	BOS	MLB	30	0.77	1.60	3.57	0.5	98.3	62.6	17.3	45.8
2019	BOS	MLB	31	1.32	4.20	4.58	0.3	97.4	62.2	17.2	45.5

Ryan Brasier, continued

Pitch Shape vs LHH

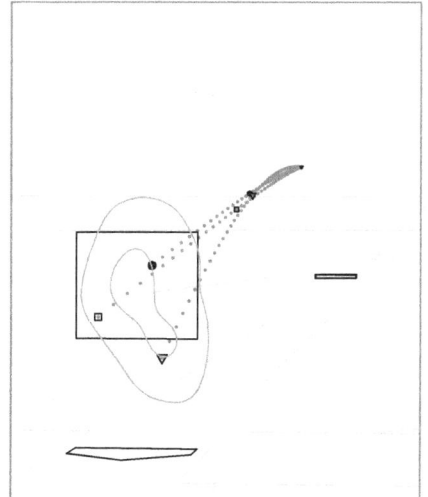

Pitch Shape vs RHH

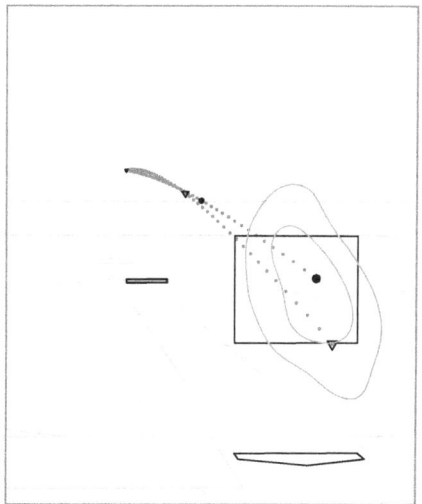

Type		Frequency	Velocity	H Movement	V Movement
●	Fastball	51.9%	97 [115]	-4.4 [110]	-11.2 [114]
☐	Sinker	10.7%	97.1 [123]	-12.3 [103]	-15.2 [117]
+	Cutter				
▲	Changeup	3.7%	88.7 [114]	-11.3 [100]	-28.2 [97]
×	Splitter				
▽	Slider	33.7%	85.6 [105]	6.3 [106]	-34.9 [94]
◇	Curveball				
⊕	Slow Curveball				
✳	Knuckleball				
▼	Screwball				

Nathan Eovaldi RHP
Born: 02/13/90 Age: 29 Bats: R Throws: R
Height: 6'2" Weight: 225 Origin: Round 11, 2008 Draft (#337 overall)

YEAR	TEAM	LVL	AGE	W	L	SV	G	GS	IP	H	HR	BB/9	K/9	K	GB%	BABIP
2016	NYA	MLB	26	9	8	0	24	21	124^2	123	23	2.9	7.0	97	50%	.275
2018	TBA	MLB	28	3	4	0	10	10	57	48	11	1.3	8.4	53	48%	.245
2018	BOS	MLB	28	3	3	0	12	11	54	57	3	2.0	8.0	48	46%	.325
2019	BOS	MLB	29	10	8	0	26	26	148	155	21	2.7	8.0	132	46%	.304

Breakout: 13%   Improve: 34%   Collapse: 25%   Attrition: 8%   MLB: 99%
Comparables: Joe Blanton, Rick Porcello, Hyun-jin Ryu

Pretty much every year, we end up talking about how Impending Free Agent X made himself a ton of money by performing well in the postseason. It's a narrative that tends to get overblown, but in Eovaldi's case it ended up being very real. Coming off of his second Tommy John surgery, Eovaldi quietly pitched really well in the season's first half, earning a July ticket to Boston, where he finally saw his pop-up stat boxes match his deserved contributions. That alone probably would've been enough to land him a two- or three-year pact in a down year for free agent pitching options, but what "Nasty Nate" did in October is truly the stuff of legend. Eovaldi made two starts and four relief appearances in Boston's 13 postseason matchups, allowing just four earned runs in 22.1 frequently-dominant innings. In Game 3 of the World Series, Eovaldi threw 97 pitches over six innings of shutout ball in relief before finally running out of gas and coughing up a walk-off homer to Max Muncy in the bottom of the 18th. Oh yeah, Eovaldi had already pitched in Games 1 and 2, and did we mention this was a guy coming off his second TJ? Clearly the Red Sox didn't see Eovaldi's excessive postseason work as a negative, even in light of those arm issues, as he'll now make big-boy money for the next four years in New England.

YEAR	TEAM	LVL	AGE	WHIP	ERA	DRA	WARP	MPH	FB%	WHF	CSP
2016	NYA	MLB	26	1.31	4.76	5.08	0.4	99.9	48.3	10.6	49.1
2018	TBA	MLB	28	0.98	4.26	3.19	1.4	98.5	38.2	12.7	54.7
2018	BOS	MLB	28	1.28	3.33	3.28	1.3	99.3	38.2	10.9	51.7
2019	BOS	MLB	29	1.37	4.06	4.54	1.5	98.6	42.3	11.3	51.7

Nathan Eovaldi, continued

Pitch Shape vs LHH

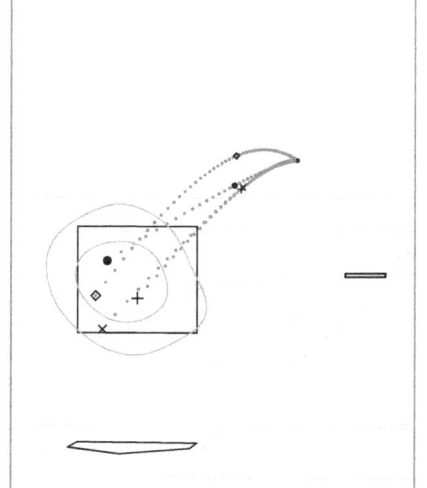

Pitch Shape vs RHH

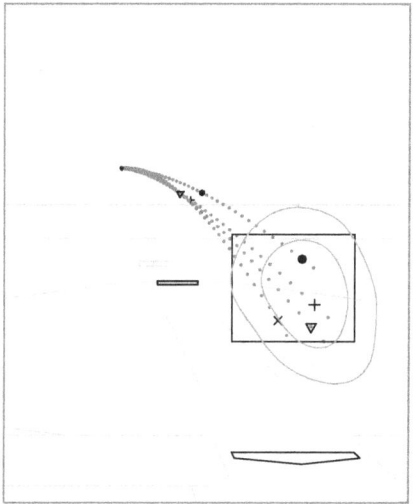

Type	Frequency	Velocity	H Movement	V Movement
● Fastball	39.7%	97.5 [116]	-9.8 [85]	-13.6 [107]
☐ Sinker	0.2%	96.1 [118]	-12.1 [104]	-20 [101]
+ Cutter	32.3%	93 [125]	1.7 [99]	-20.3 [114]
▲ Changeup				
✕ Splitter	12.8%	88.5 [116]	-8.7 [98]	-29.2 [101]
▽ Slider	11.5%	86.9 [111]	4.1 [97]	-30.2 [108]
◇ Curveball	3.4%	79 [102]	6.9 [96]	-48.7 [99]
⊕ Slow Curveball				
✶ Knuckleball				
▼ Screwball				

Heath Hembree RHP

Born: 01/13/89   Age: 30   Bats: R   Throws: R
Height: 6'4"   Weight: 210   Origin: Round 5, 2010 Draft (#168 overall)

YEAR	TEAM	LVL	AGE	W	L	SV	G	GS	IP	H	HR	BB/9	K/9	K	GB%	BABIP
2016	PAW	AAA	27	0	0	8	13	0	13¹	6	0	2.0	14.9	22	38%	.250
2016	BOS	MLB	27	4	1	0	38	0	51	51	6	3.0	8.3	47	38%	.294
2017	BOS	MLB	28	2	3	0	62	0	62	72	10	2.6	10.2	70	42%	.360
2018	BOS	MLB	29	4	1	0	67	0	60	53	10	4.1	11.4	76	40%	.295
2019	BOS	MLB	30	3	3	3	53	0	55	52	7	3.6	9.8	61	40%	.299

Breakout: 19%   Improve: 47%   Collapse: 21%   Attrition: 17%   MLB: 83%
Comparables: Fernando Abad, David Carpenter, Junichi Tazawa

No pitcher better represents 2018 than Heath Hembree. He posted a 4.20 ERA, right on the nose. He struck out a ton of batters and gave up a ton of home runs. Plus, Hembree doesn't just look like Kenny Powers; he acts like him, too. When asked if he'd be visiting the White House post-World Series win, he replied "Hell Yeah! I F*** with Trump!" When asked what he likes best about the President, Hembree gave a thoughtful, measured response: "Everything!" There is a 90 percent chance Hembree believed Pizzagate. He's probably still worried about The Caravan. Unlike his voter-suppressing party, he still can't get lefties out. What a stupid time to be alive.

YEAR	TEAM	LVL	AGE	WHIP	ERA	DRA	WARP	MPH	FB%	WHF	CSP
2016	PAW	AAA	27	0.68	0.68	2.23	0.4				
2016	BOS	MLB	27	1.33	2.65	4.92	0.0	96.5	60.4	10.4	52
2017	BOS	MLB	28	1.45	3.63	3.39	1.2	97.4	53.1	15.2	45.3
2018	BOS	MLB	29	1.33	4.20	3.87	0.7	96.6	54.9	15.5	45.3
2019	BOS	MLB	30	1.33	3.59	4.07	0.7	96.1	55.2	14.3	46.8

Heath Hembree, continued

Pitch Shape vs LHH

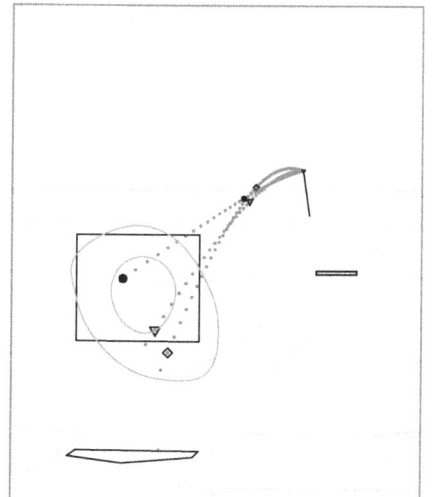

Pitch Shape vs RHH

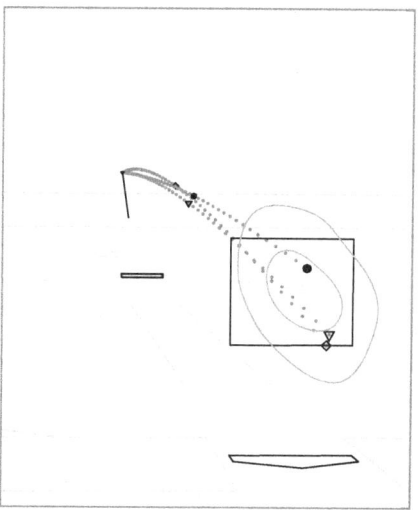

Type	Frequency	Velocity	H Movement	V Movement
● Fastball	54.9%	94.9 [108]	-5.1 [107]	-11.9 [112]
☐ Sinker				
+ Cutter				
▲ Changeup				
✕ Splitter				
▽ Slider	34.1%	89.2 [121]	4.4 [98]	-26.4 [119]
◇ Curveball	11.0%	82.1 [113]	8.9 [105]	-42.7 [112]
✥ Slow Curveball				
✳ Knuckleball				
▼ Screwball				

Brian Johnson LHP
Born: 12/07/90 Age: 28 Bats: L Throws: L
Height: 6'4" Weight: 235 Origin: Round 1, 2012 Draft (#31 overall)

YEAR	TEAM	LVL	AGE	W	L	SV	G	GS	IP	H	HR	BB/9	K/9	K	GB%	BABIP
2016	LOW	A-	25	0	0	0	2	2	11	7	0	1.6	9.0	11	37%	.259
2016	PAW	AAA	25	5	6	0	15	15	77	74	9	4.2	6.3	54	36%	.284
2017	BOS	MLB	26	2	0	0	5	5	27	32	5	2.7	7.0	21	38%	.310
2017	PAW	AAA	26	3	4	0	17	17	90^1	82	10	2.8	7.0	70	39%	.271
2018	BOS	MLB	27	4	5	0	38	13	99^1	104	16	3.4	7.9	87	38%	.301
2019	BOS	MLB	28	5	5	0	35	11	80	82	13	3.8	7.6	68	38%	.290

Breakout: 12% Improve: 24% Collapse: 13% Attrition: 24% MLB: 53%
Comparables: Allen Webster, Logan Verrett, Kyle Lobstein

Life has not been terribly fair to Johnson since the Red Sox drafted him in the first round in 2012. A batted ball broke his face shortly after his professional debut. Shoulder and elbow injuries hampered him at various points. He's missed time with an anxiety disorder. Hell, he was even car-jacked at gunpoint back in 2016. We can all take some measure of happiness, then, in Johnson winning a ring in 2018. For the first time in his career, Johnson spent the entire season in the majors. He performed exactly as expected—not well, despite a decent looking ERA—while occupying the swingman role for the Red Sox, at some points serving as their primary southpaw out of the 'pen. This may very well be Johnson's ceiling, but at the same time it also seems like his floor.

YEAR	TEAM	LVL	AGE	WHIP	ERA	DRA	WARP	MPH	FB%	WHF	CSP
2016	LOW	A-	25	0.82	0.00	3.57	0.2				
2016	PAW	AAA	25	1.43	4.09	5.93	-0.5				
2017	BOS	MLB	26	1.48	4.33	5.98	-0.1	89.8	55.9	8.5	44.1
2017	PAW	AAA	26	1.22	3.09	5.25	0.5				
2018	BOS	MLB	27	1.43	4.17	6.16	-1.1	91.1	49	9.5	47
2019	BOS	MLB	28	1.42	4.91	5.29	0.0	90.3	50.5	9.4	46

Brian Johnson, continued

Pitch Shape vs LHH

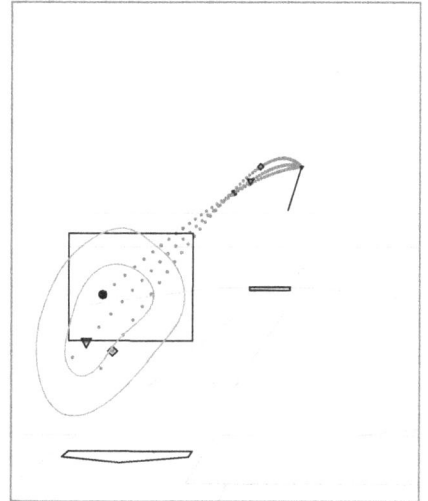

Pitch Shape vs RHH

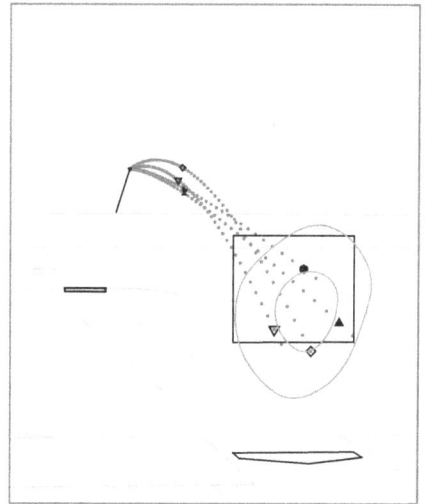

Type	Frequency	Velocity	H Movement	V Movement
● Fastball	47.5%	88.8 [88]	5 [108]	-16.2 [98]
☐ Sinker	1.5%	89 [83]	12.6 [100]	-19.2 [104]
+ Cutter				
▲ Changeup	1.9%	81.8 [86]	8.9 [113]	-24.2 [109]
✕ Splitter				
▽ Slider	19.8%	78.6 [74]	-9.6 [121]	-39.8 [80]
◇ Curveball	29.3%	75 [87]	-8.2 [101]	-55.9 [82]
⊕ Slow Curveball				
✱ Knuckleball				
▼ Screwball				

Boston Red Sox 2019

Rick Porcello   RHP
Born: 12/27/88   Age: 30   Bats: R   Throws: R
Height: 6'5"   Weight: 205   Origin: Round 1, 2007 Draft (#27 overall)

YEAR	TEAM	LVL	AGE	W	L	SV	G	GS	IP	H	HR	BB/9	K/9	K	GB%	BABIP
2016	BOS	MLB	27	22	4	0	33	33	223	193	23	1.3	7.6	189	44%	.269
2017	BOS	MLB	28	11	17	0	33	33	203^1	236	38	2.1	8.0	181	40%	.322
2018	BOS	MLB	29	17	7	0	33	33	191^1	177	27	2.3	8.9	190	45%	.285
2019	BOS	MLB	30	12	8	0	28	28	168	167	22	2.3	7.7	144	43%	.296

Breakout: 11%   Improve: 47%   Collapse: 20%   Attrition: 5%   MLB: 96%
Comparables: Don Drysdale, Wade Miley, Cliff Lee

Porcello finally found the middle of the bell curve. In 2015, Porcello's first year with the Red Sox, he was terrible. In 2016, he won the Cy Young. In 2017, he was pretty bad. But in 2018, Pretty Ricky was the C+/B- version of himself, a guy whose results finally seemed to mesh with his stuff. There are three primary reasons Porcello got better last year. First, he did a better job keeping the ball in the yard, even if "better" still put him in a league with Kevin Gausman, Jason Hammel and Mike Wright. Second, Porcello threw his fastball and sinker a little less and his slider a little more, a mix that led to a career-best strikeout rate. Finally—and perhaps most importantly—he just had better luck. Porcello's 2017 BABIP and homer rates were always the good kind of unsustainable, and as they fell back to league average, so too did Porcello. Factor in some postseason heroics out of the bullpen and all things considered, Porcello had a really nice year. Whether he'll be great, average or terrible again in 2019 is anyone's guess.

YEAR	TEAM	LVL	AGE	WHIP	ERA	DRA	WARP	MPH	FB%	WHF	CSP
2016	BOS	MLB	27	1.01	3.15	3.37	5.1	93.9	62.1	8.9	49.6
2017	BOS	MLB	28	1.40	4.65	4.84	1.7	93.9	59.4	10.4	49.1
2018	BOS	MLB	29	1.18	4.28	4.02	2.8	92.8	50	9.6	48.9
2019	BOS	MLB	30	1.25	3.88	4.34	2.1	92.7	56.2	9.7	49

Rick Porcello, continued

Pitch Shape vs LHH

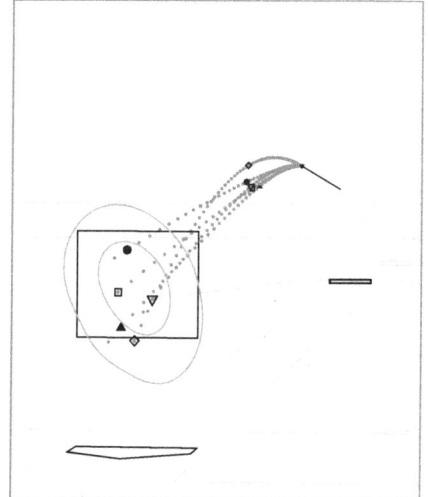

Pitch Shape vs RHH

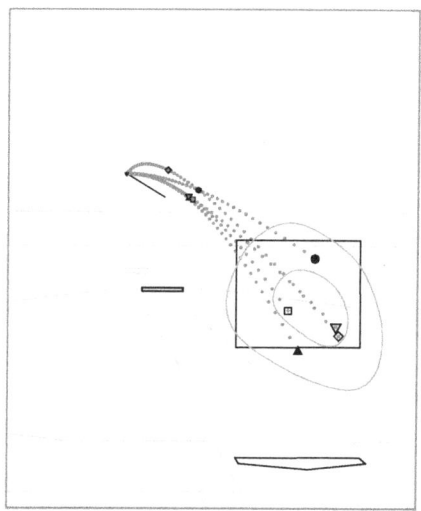

Type		Frequency	Velocity	H Movement	V Movement
●	Fastball	21.1%	91.7 [97]	-7.1 [98]	-15 [102]
□	Sinker	28.9%	90.2 [89]	-13.9 [89]	-22.1 [94]
+	Cutter				
▲	Changeup	11.7%	81.9 [86]	-13.4 [89]	-31.6 [88]
×	Splitter				
▽	Slider	24.3%	86.3 [108]	2.9 [91]	-27.2 [117]
◇	Curveball	14.0%	75 [87]	14.2 [127]	-52.8 [89]
⊕	Slow Curveball				
✳	Knuckleball				
▼	Screwball				

David Price LHP

Born: 08/26/85 Age: 33 Bats: L Throws: L
Height: 6'5" Weight: 215 Origin: Round 1, 2007 Draft (#1 overall)

YEAR	TEAM	LVL	AGE	W	L	SV	G	GS	IP	H	HR	BB/9	K/9	K	GB%	BABIP
2016	BOS	MLB	30	17	9	0	35	35	230	227	30	2.0	8.9	228	45%	.310
2017	BOS	MLB	31	6	3	0	16	11	74^2	65	8	2.9	9.2	76	40%	.278
2018	BOS	MLB	32	16	7	0	30	30	176	151	25	2.6	9.1	177	41%	.274
2019	BOS	MLB	33	11	8	0	27	27	162	160	22	2.7	8.4	151	42%	.297

Breakout: 11% Improve: 34% Collapse: 34% Attrition: 18% MLB: 92%
Comparables: Johan Santana, Josh Beckett, Cole Hamels

If you sent a script outlining Price's postseason redemption arc to Hollywood, it'd get rejected as a fairy tale. Even as recently as October 6, it seemed unfathomable that we'd be talking about David Price: Postseason Hero. Price had just lost Game 2 of the ALDS against the Yankees, lasting only 1 2/3 innings while dropping his all-time playoff record to 0-10 with an ERA above 5.00. Had Alex Cora and Co. decided to withhold him from any further playoff starts, they wouldn't have received much pushback.

But Cora ignored the narrative, the small sample size and the noise, and trusted talent instead. Price got the nod to start ALCS Game 2 and held his own against a tough Astros lineup, earning a standing ovation from the Fenway Faithful despite pitching just 4.2 innings. Price took the ball again four days later and tossed an absolute gem in Game 5, holding Houston scoreless through six innings for his first playoff win. Add in two more outstanding World Series starts and one clutch relief appearance, and Price transformed from scapegoat to Boston's best overall postseason performer this side of Nate Eovaldi.

Make no mistake about it; many of the Sox fans who are singing his praises now will be quick to decry him once more if he struggles. That's especially true now that Price will make nearly $32 million per season over the next four years after declining his opt-out. But for the moment, let's all appreciate that the much-maligned Price has finally been accepted by his fan base, and that one of the best left-handers of his generation removed a King Kong-sized monkey from his back. Your move, Clayton!

YEAR	TEAM	LVL	AGE	WHIP	ERA	DRA	WARP	MPH	FB%	WHF	CSP
2016	BOS	MLB	30	1.20	3.99	3.13	5.9	95.5	48.7	12.7	48.7
2017	BOS	MLB	31	1.19	3.38	5.04	0.4	96.0	58.3	13.1	44.1
2018	BOS	MLB	32	1.14	3.58	3.72	3.2	94.2	46.5	10.8	49.9
2019	BOS	MLB	33	1.29	3.92	4.38	2.0	93.9	48.7	11.7	47.1

David Price, continued

Pitch Shape vs LHH

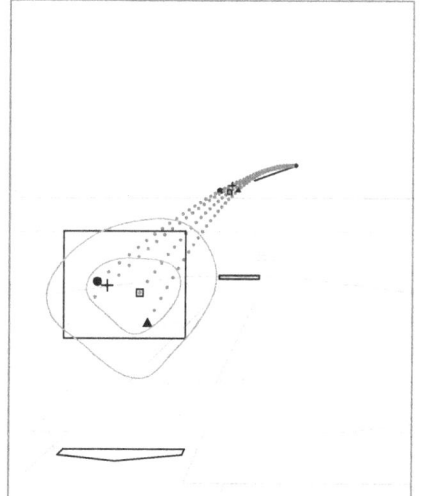

Pitch Shape vs RHH

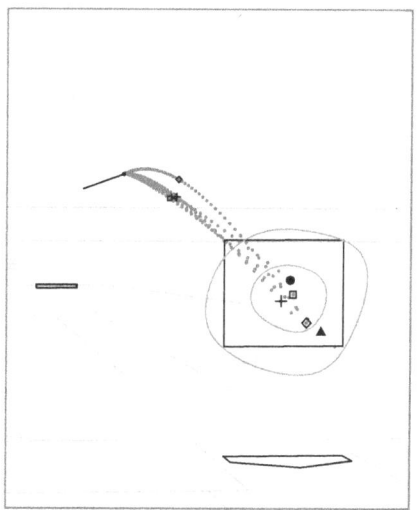

Type	Frequency	Velocity	H Movement	V Movement
● Fastball	13.2%	93.1 [102]	8.4 [92]	-15.6 [100]
☐ Sinker	33.3%	93.1 [103]	14.4 [85]	-18.6 [106]
+ Cutter	28.4%	89 [101]	0.5 [86]	-22.8 [104]
▲ Changeup	22.2%	85.5 [101]	14.4 [84]	-28.2 [98]
✕ Splitter				
▽ Slider				
◇ Curveball	2.9%	79.4 [104]	-5.6 [90]	-40 [118]
✦ Slow Curveball				
✱ Knuckleball				
▼ Screwball				

Erasmo Ramirez RHP

Born: 05/02/90 Age: 29 Bats: R Throws: R
Height: 5'10" Weight: 215 Origin: International Free Agent, 2007

YEAR	TEAM	LVL	AGE	W	L	SV	G	GS	IP	H	HR	BB/9	K/9	K	GB%	BABIP
2016	TBA	MLB	26	7	11	2	64	1	90^2	90	14	2.6	6.3	63	55%	.280
2017	TBA	MLB	27	4	3	1	26	8	69^1	66	10	2.1	7.1	55	49%	.280
2017	SEA	MLB	27	1	3	0	11	11	62	57	12	2.2	7.8	54	39%	.257
2018	TAC	AAA	28	0	2	0	5	5	18^2	14	1	1.4	8.2	17	46%	.245
2018	SEA	MLB	28	2	4	0	10	10	45^2	52	14	2.4	6.5	33	40%	.271
2019	BOS	MLB	29	1	1	0	12	2	20	20	3	3.0	6.9	16	45%	.292

Breakout: 34% Improve: 49% Collapse: 24% Attrition: 13% MLB: 93%
Comparables: Jae Weong Seo, Wade Miley, Dave Bush

One of the encouraging trends in baseball the past few years has been the move away from the baseball player as spreadsheet abstraction, and towards a more humanistic, holistic appraisal of the men in uniform. As such, when a player suffers a poor game, week, month, or season, it is no longer en vogue to take turns slinging acerbic witticisms. Instead, perhaps, our better angels demand we consider the truth of all baseball players: They are human, and they try hard. When discussing Ramirez's 2018, it is probably best if we acknowledge those two facts, and, in absence of anything else positive to say, move on to 2019.

YEAR	TEAM	LVL	AGE	WHIP	ERA	DRA	WARP	MPH	FB%	WHF	CSP
2016	TBA	MLB	26	1.28	3.77	4.48	0.5	94.3	63	9.9	48
2017	TBA	MLB	27	1.18	4.80	4.23	1.0	93.2	42.2	11	51.5
2017	SEA	MLB	27	1.16	3.92	4.52	0.7	93.4	42.2	10.6	45.3
2018	TAC	AAA	28	0.91	2.41	3.85	0.4				
2018	SEA	MLB	28	1.40	6.50	6.55	-0.7	91.6	40.8	9.6	49.4
2019	BOS	MLB	29	1.34	4.54	4.91	0.1	92.5	47.1	10.3	48.8

Erasmo Ramirez, continued

Pitch Shape vs LHH

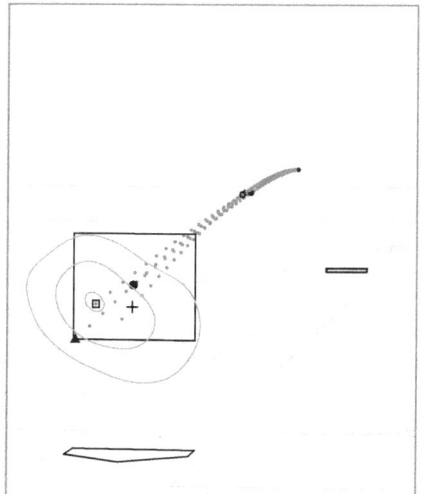

Pitch Shape vs RHH

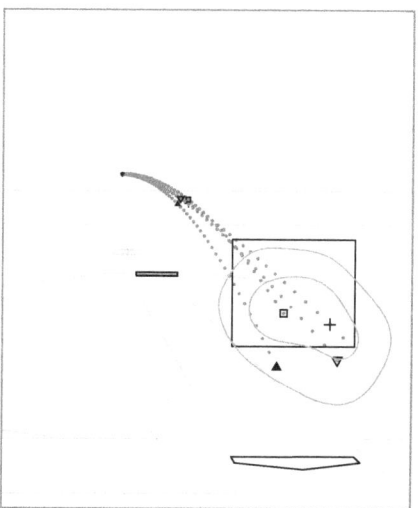

Type	Frequency	Velocity	H Movement	V Movement
● Fastball	8.9%	90.9 [95]	-7.4 [96]	-16.6 [97]
☐ Sinker	31.9%	90.2 [89]	-13 [97]	-23 [91]
+ Cutter	27.5%	86.6 [87]	2.6 [104]	-22.7 [104]
▲ Changeup	19.5%	82.8 [90]	-11.7 [97]	-29.2 [94]
✕ Splitter				
▽ Slider	10.9%	81.6 [87]	5.3 [102]	-34.8 [95]
◇ Curveball	1.2%	75.3 [88]	7.3 [98]	-47.5 [101]
✣ Slow Curveball				
✱ Knuckleball				
▼ Screwball				

Eduardo Rodriguez LHP

Born: 04/07/93 Age: 26 Bats: L Throws: L
Height: 6'2" Weight: 220 Origin: International Free Agent, 2010

YEAR	TEAM	LVL	AGE	W	L	SV	G	GS	IP	H	HR	BB/9	K/9	K	GB%	BABIP
2016	PAW	AAA	23	0	4	0	7	7	38	33	6	1.7	5.7	24	43%	.233
2016	BOS	MLB	23	3	7	0	20	20	107	99	16	3.4	8.4	100	33%	.278
2017	PAW	AAA	24	0	1	0	2	2	10^1	10	0	4.4	10.5	12	38%	.385
2017	BOS	MLB	24	6	7	0	25	24	137^1	126	19	3.3	9.8	150	36%	.299
2018	BOS	MLB	25	13	5	0	27	23	129^2	119	16	3.1	10.1	146	39%	.301
2019	BOS	MLB	26	9	6	0	23	23	131	121	16	3.2	9.4	137	38%	.295

Breakout: 29% Improve: 67% Collapse: 16% Attrition: 8% MLB: 96%
Comparables: Matt Garza, Tyler Skaggs, Kevin Gausman

Few people should be happier that the Red Sox won the World Series than Rodriguez, not just because of the ring and the history and playoff shares, but because he may have avoided infamy. Had the Dodgers prevailed, the image of Yasiel Puig triumphantly raising his hands as Rodriguez slammed his glove in the dirt after allowing a three-run homer in Game 4 might've gone down as one of the most iconic in postseason history. Instead, it's just a footnote in what was a wildly successful season for the Sox but yet another injury-marred one for Rodriguez. Rodriguez started the year strong enough after off-season knee surgery, posting a 3.44 ERA and striking out more than a batter per inning in his first 19 starts. But on July 15, E-Rod damaged the ligament in his ankle in a collision at first base, keeping him off the mound until September. The Sox tried to move him to the bullpen for their postseason run, but he was largely ineffective and he looked to be pitching hurt. Overall, it's a familiar tale for Rodriguez, who has the talent to become a mid-rotation mainstay but the overall leg integrity of an AT-AT. But hey, at least he avoided becoming a meme.

YEAR	TEAM	LVL	AGE	WHIP	ERA	DRA	WARP	MPH	FB%	WHF	CSP
2016	PAW	AAA	23	1.05	3.08	3.52	0.8				
2016	BOS	MLB	23	1.30	4.71	5.81	-0.5	96.1	66.3	11.7	43.8
2017	PAW	AAA	24	1.45	4.35	3.36	0.3				
2017	BOS	MLB	24	1.28	4.19	4.37	1.8	95.0	65.3	12.4	44
2018	BOS	MLB	25	1.26	3.82	3.77	2.3	95.1	51.6	12.4	46.4
2019	BOS	MLB	26	1.29	3.70	4.13	2.0	94.9	60.7	12.5	45.8

Eduardo Rodriguez, continued

Pitch Shape vs LHH

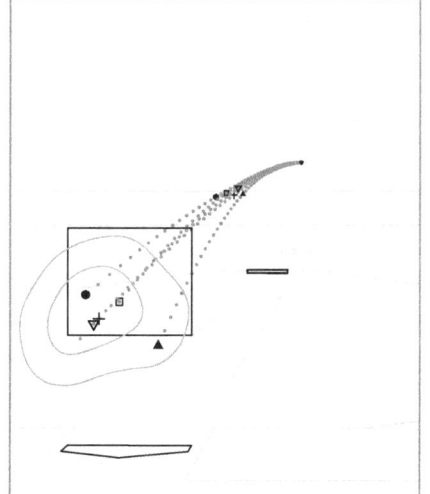

Pitch Shape vs RHH

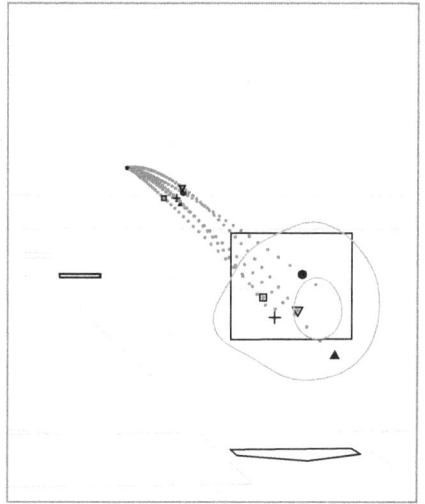

Type	Frequency	Velocity	H Movement	V Movement
● Fastball	42.0%	93.6 [104]	9.5 [87]	-15.6 [100]
☐ Sinker	9.6%	93.5 [105]	15 [80]	-19.1 [104]
+ Cutter	15.5%	89.3 [103]	0.7 [85]	-22.6 [105]
▲ Changeup	21.1%	87.8 [110]	16.5 [72]	-27.5 [100]
✕ Splitter				
▽ Slider	11.8%	85.4 [104]	-1.2 [84]	-28.7 [113]
◇ Curveball				
✥ Slow Curveball				
✳ Knuckleball				
▼ Screwball				

Chris Sale LHP

Born: 03/30/89 Age: 30 Bats: L Throws: L
Height: 6'6" Weight: 180 Origin: Round 1, 2010 Draft (#13 overall)

YEAR	TEAM	LVL	AGE	W	L	SV	G	GS	IP	H	HR	BB/9	K/9	K	GB%	BABIP
2016	CHA	MLB	27	17	10	0	32	32	226^2	190	27	1.8	9.3	233	42%	.279
2017	BOS	MLB	28	17	8	0	32	32	214^1	165	24	1.8	12.9	308	40%	.301
2018	BOS	MLB	29	12	4	0	27	27	158	102	11	1.9	13.5	237	45%	.283
2019	BOS	MLB	30	14	6	0	28	28	176	138	16	2.2	11.6	227	42%	.296

Breakout: 16% Improve: 48% Collapse: 19% Attrition: 8% MLB: 95%
Comparables: Yu Darvish, David Price, Ron Guidry

When Sale is at his best, he's the most dominant pitcher in baseball. Let's take his first 11 starts of 2018, for example: He posted a 2.17 ERA, struck out 96 batters in 70 2/3 innings and held batters to a .187/.252/.333 line. He started the All-Star game for the third straight year, and was in the catbird seat for his first-ever Cy Young award through the season's first half. But, as is often the case, Sale faded down the stretch. This time it was shoulder fatigue that derailed Sale's run, as the Sox put him on the DL twice due to his ailing joint. When he finally returned for good in September, Sale clearly wasn't himself, with diminished velocity and spotty command limiting his effectiveness even in short stints. Despite pitching at less than 100 percent, Sale enjoyed a solid postseason, gutting out three solid (albeit short) starts and two relief appearances, including the World Series-clinching ninth inning of Game 5. Sale is now entering his walk year, and there's an argument that a talent of his age (he'll turn 30 in March) and track record should threaten the record books when it comes to starting pitcher contracts. But given his whippet-thin frame, jerky delivery and history of relative second-half declines, Sale may fail to reach Kershaw-ian heights. That's putting the cart a bit before the horse, however, and for now Sale can keep his eye on a more immediate prize of helping the Sox repeat as World Champions.

YEAR	TEAM	LVL	AGE	WHIP	ERA	DRA	WARP	MPH	FB%	WHF	CSP
2016	CHA	MLB	27	1.04	3.34	3.13	5.8	97.0	60.9	12.2	49.3
2017	BOS	MLB	28	0.97	2.90	2.51	7.3	97.4	50.5	15.8	48.3
2018	BOS	MLB	29	0.86	2.11	2.24	5.6	99.1	50.1	16.9	49.4
2019	BOS	MLB	30	1.03	2.51	2.86	5.3	97.1	53.1	15.1	48.9

Chris Sale, continued

Pitch Shape vs LHH

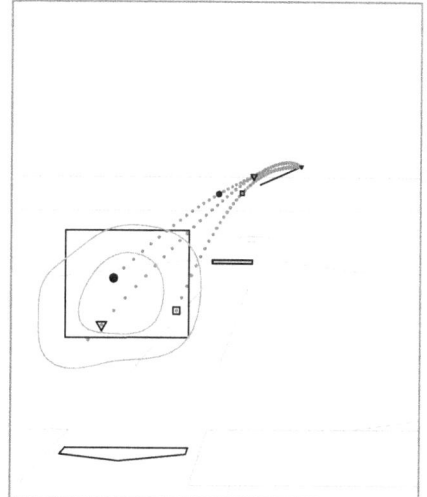

Pitch Shape vs RHH

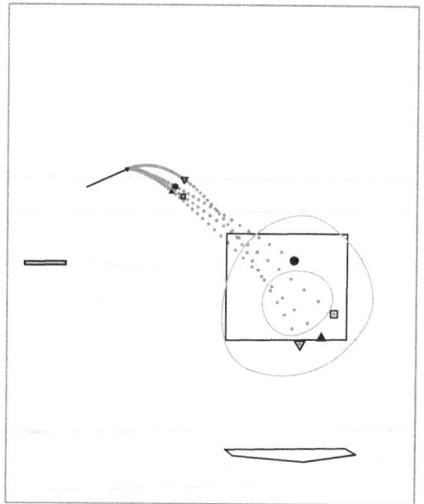

Type	Frequency	Velocity	H Movement	V Movement
● Fastball	38.9%	95.7 [110]	13.2 [70]	-16.7 [97]
☐ Sinker	11.1%	93.1 [103]	17.6 [58]	-25 [85]
+ Cutter				
▲ Changeup	15.4%	87.3 [108]	17.4 [68]	-32.4 [85]
✕ Splitter				
▽ Slider	34.5%	80.1 [80]	-11.9 [130]	-42.2 [73]
◇ Curveball				
⊕ Slow Curveball				
✱ Knuckleball				
▼ Screwball				

Carson Smith RHP

Born: 10/19/89 Age: 29 Bats: R Throws: R
Height: 6'6" Weight: 215 Origin: Round 8, 2011 Draft (#243 overall)

YEAR	TEAM	LVL	AGE	W	L	SV	G	GS	IP	H	HR	BB/9	K/9	K	GB%	BABIP
2016	BOS	MLB	26	0	0	0	3	0	2^2	2	0	3.4	6.8	2	75%	.250
2017	BOS	MLB	27	0	0	1	8	0	6^2	7	0	2.7	9.4	7	61%	.389
2018	BOS	MLB	28	1	1	0	18	0	14^1	14	2	3.8	11.3	18	55%	.316
2019	BOS	MLB	29	2	1	1	32	0	34	31	3	4.8	9.4	35	49%	.304

Breakout: 22% Improve: 39% Collapse: 31% Attrition: 20% MLB: 88%
Comparables: Ryan Cook, Hunter Strickland, A.J. Ramos

After missing most of 2017 recovering from Tommy John, Smith was okay-ish in 18 outings before three very bad throws derailed his season. The first one came on May 14, when Smith gave up a bomb to Khris Davis. The second one also came on May 14, when Smith hurt his shoulder chucking his glove in the dugout immediately after surrendering said Khrushjob. And the third bad toss? That came in mid-June, when Smith attempted to hurl Alex Cora under the bus, blaming overuse for his shoulder malady instead of, ya know, the whole glove-related temper tantrum. Smith eventually needed surgery to repair his labrum, and it's a toss-up as to whether he'll be ready for the start of 2019. The way those have gone for Smith lately it's hard to be very optimistic.

YEAR	TEAM	LVL	AGE	WHIP	ERA	DRA	WARP	MPH	FB%	WHF	CSP
2016	BOS	MLB	26	1.12	0.00	6.73	-0.1	94.5	52.1	4.2	48.3
2017	BOS	MLB	27	1.35	1.35	3.42	0.1	93.5	49.1	9.7	51.5
2018	BOS	MLB	28	1.40	3.77	4.04	0.1	93.7	50.2	12.2	47.3
2019	BOS	MLB	29	1.46	4.16	4.38	0.2	93.1	50.1	11	49

Carson Smith, continued

Pitch Shape vs LHH

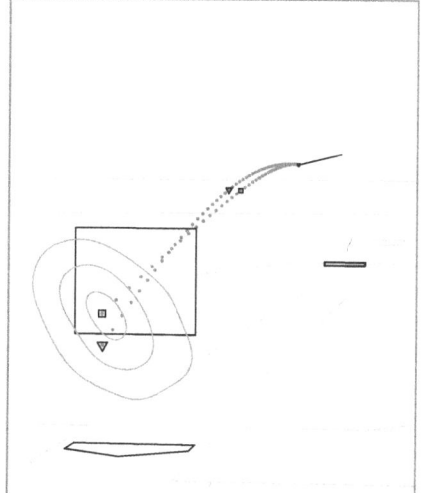

Pitch Shape vs RHH

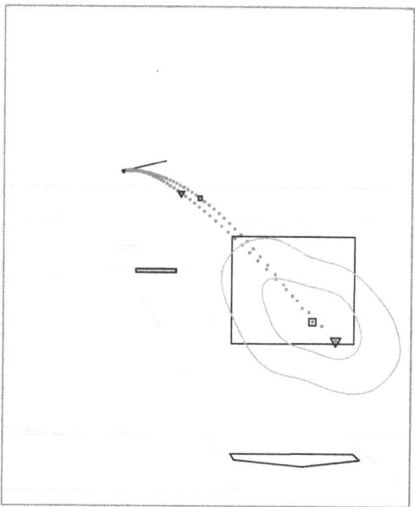

Type	Frequency	Velocity	H Movement	V Movement
● Fastball	0.8%	93.8 [104]	-12.4 [74]	-19.3 [89]
□ Sinker	49.4%	92.5 [100]	-12.7 [99]	-27.6 [76]
+ Cutter				
▲ Changeup	6.1%	90.1 [119]	-12.3 [95]	-33.3 [82]
× Splitter				
▽ Slider	43.7%	85.7 [106]	9.9 [122]	-34.7 [95]
◇ Curveball				
⊕ Slow Curveball				
✳ Knuckleball				
▼ Screwball				

Tyler Thornburg RHP

Born: 09/29/88 Age: 30 Bats: R Throws: R
Height: 5'11" Weight: 190 Origin: Round 3, 2010 Draft (#96 overall)

YEAR	TEAM	LVL	AGE	W	L	SV	G	GS	IP	H	HR	BB/9	K/9	K	GB%	BABIP
2016	MIL	MLB	27	8	5	13	67	0	67	38	6	3.4	12.1	90	36%	.229
2018	PAW	AAA	29	0	1	0	15	1	12²	11	3	4.3	7.8	11	20%	.216
2018	BOS	MLB	29	2	0	0	25	0	24	28	6	3.8	7.9	21	37%	.319
2019	BOS	MLB	30	2	2	0	38	0	40²	39	6	4.0	8.5	38	37%	.288

Breakout: 16% Improve: 34% Collapse: 18% Attrition: 18% MLB: 66%
Comparables: Angel Guzman, Wesley Wright, Chris Resop

By the time this book is published, it will have been more than two years since Dave Dombrowski traded Travis Shaw and some prospects to the Brewers for Thornburg. To date, it's a move that's cost the Red Sox about nine wins, per WARP. Thornburg finally threw his first pitch for Boston on July 6, a year-plus removed from thoracic outlet surgery on his right shoulder. In that debut outing Thornburg gave up a run to the lowly Royals, and his season didn't get better from there. The 29-year-old's velocity was down from his halcyon days of 2016, and while his breaking stuff occasionally had some bite to it, his fastball looked flat and his command went AWOL. The Sox shut Thornburg down for the season in late September with the hope that a full, healthy offseason gets him right. If not, the Thornburg deal will continue reading as a cautionary tale about trading for relief pitching.

YEAR	TEAM	LVL	AGE	WHIP	ERA	DRA	WARP	MPH	FB%	WHF	CSP
2016	MIL	MLB	27	0.94	2.15	3.05	1.5	96.4	66.3	13	46.9
2018	PAW	AAA	29	1.34	4.26	4.45	0.1				
2018	BOS	MLB	29	1.58	5.62	5.01	0.0	94.4	55.6	9.5	46.2
2019	BOS	MLB	30	1.40	4.79	5.04	0.1	94.9	61.9	11.6	46.3

Tyler Thornburg, continued

Pitch Shape vs LHH

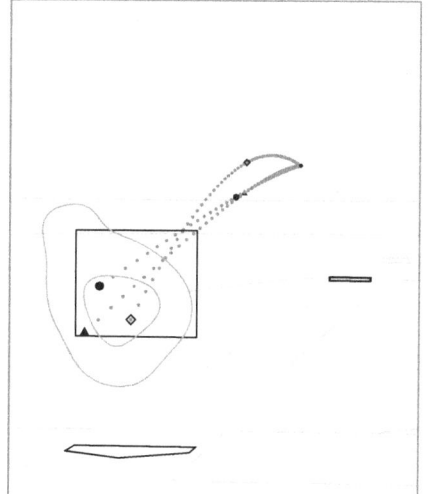

Pitch Shape vs RHH

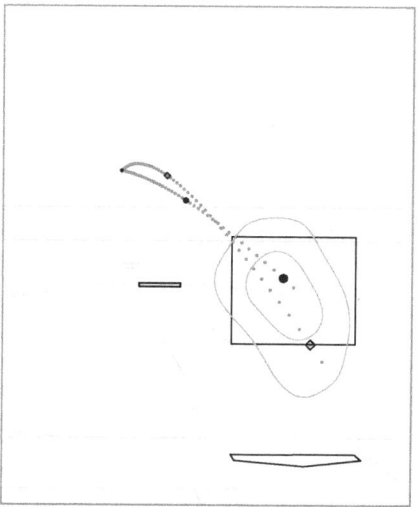

Type	Frequency	Velocity	H Movement	V Movement
● Fastball	55.6%	93.1 [102]	-5.5 [106]	-11.3 [114]
☐ Sinker				
+ Cutter				
▲ Changeup	15.1%	85 [99]	-9.7 [109]	-24.5 [109]
✕ Splitter				
▽ Slider				
◇ Curveball	29.3%	78 [98]	9.6 [108]	-51.8 [92]
✦ Slow Curveball				
✱ Knuckleball				
▼ Screwball				

Hector Velazquez RHP

Born: 11/26/88 Age: 30 Bats: R Throws: R
Height: 6'0" Weight: 180 Origin: International Free Agent, 2017

YEAR	TEAM	LVL	AGE	W	L	SV	G	GS	IP	H	HR	BB/9	K/9	K	GB%	BABIP
2017	PAW	AAA	28	8	4	0	19	19	102	78	7	2.1	7.0	79	45%	.251
2017	BOS	MLB	28	3	1	0	8	3	24^2	21	4	2.6	6.9	19	44%	.258
2018	BOS	MLB	29	7	2	0	47	8	85	97	7	2.8	5.6	53	50%	.325
2019	BOS	MLB	30	4	4	0	42	8	75	81	11	3.0	6.0	50	46%	.295

Breakout: 12% Improve: 27% Collapse: 21% Attrition: 20% MLB: 64%
Comparables: Christian Friedrich, Jeremy Guthrie, Clay Hensley

In an era of strikeouts, homers and premium velocity, Velazquez seems like a traveler from the past. The former Mexican Leaguer averaged just 92 mph on his fastball. He struck out a lower percentage of batters faced than Mike Leake, Andrew Cashner or Wade Miley. He had no defined role, bouncing between starter, long reliever and medium-leverage fireman—he was basically a Ray. And yet, Velazquez succeeded. He didn't walk anyone. He induced some ground balls. He did a decent job suppressing homers. All told, he threw 85 boring, unremarkable, effective innings for the World Series champions. Contributions like Velazquez's will always go unnoticed on elite teams, but collectively, they make up much of the fabric of a successful 162-game season. Seriously though, how is he not a Ray?

YEAR	TEAM	LVL	AGE	WHIP	ERA	DRA	WARP	MPH	FB%	WHF	CSP
2017	PAW	AAA	28	1.00	2.21	3.70	2.2				
2017	BOS	MLB	28	1.14	2.92	4.88	0.1	92.0	68.9	8.6	51.2
2018	BOS	MLB	29	1.45	3.18	5.61	-0.5	93.1	59.2	9	46.7
2019	BOS	MLB	30	1.41	4.79	5.14	0.1	92.1	60.8	8.9	48.5

Hector Velazquez, continued

Pitch Shape vs LHH

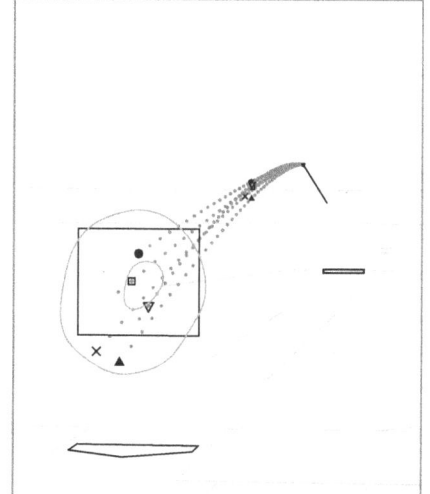

Pitch Shape vs RHH

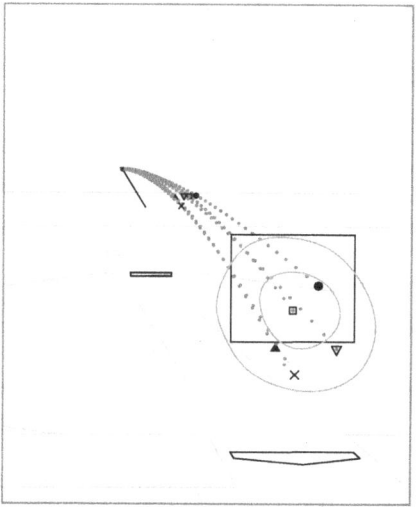

Type		Frequency	Velocity	H Movement	V Movement
●	Fastball	23.1%	92.1 [99]	-6.5 [101]	-15.2 [102]
□	Sinker	36.2%	90.7 [91]	-11.8 [107]	-21.4 [96]
+	Cutter				
▲	Changeup	7.1%	85.7 [101]	-6.4 [126]	-30.9 [89]
×	Splitter	18.2%	86 [102]	-6.9 [105]	-29.8 [99]
▽	Slider	12.2%	84.4 [100]	2.6 [90]	-29.8 [110]
◇	Curveball	3.4%	77.2 [95]	6.2 [93]	-46.3 [104]
⊕	Slow Curveball				
✳	Knuckleball				
▼	Screwball				

Brandon Workman   RHP

Born: 08/13/88 Age: 30 Bats: R Throws: R
Height: 6'5" Weight: 235 Origin: Round 2, 2010 Draft (#57 overall)

YEAR	TEAM	LVL	AGE	W	L	SV	G	GS	IP	H	HR	BB/9	K/9	K	GB%	BABIP
2016	PME	AA	27	0	0	0	4	0	10	15	3	6.3	4.5	5	48%	.324
2017	PAW	AAA	28	4	1	2	18	0	29	16	1	4.0	10.9	35	46%	.234
2017	BOS	MLB	28	1	1	0	33	0	39²	37	7	2.5	8.4	37	44%	.283
2018	PAW	AAA	29	2	1	1	17	0	30	21	3	1.5	10.2	34	40%	.247
2018	BOS	MLB	29	6	1	0	43	0	41¹	34	6	3.5	8.1	37	46%	.259
2019	BOS	MLB	30	2	3	0	48	0	50	48	7	4.1	8.6	48	43%	.288

Breakout: 11% Improve: 25% Collapse: 25% Attrition: 27% MLB: 59%
Comparables: Josh Outman, Wil Ledezma, Tyler Yates

What is the worst insult you can think of? Maybe it's a Winston Churchill quote? Or something in Piers Morgan's Twitter mentions? Or anything Peter MacNicol says to Jonah on "Veep?" Wrong; it's actually getting dropped from the World Series roster in favor of 2018 Drew Pomeranz. That indignity aside, Workman has to be fairly pleased with how his season went. He spent more than half the year in the majors, posted respectable surface-level stats and even made the postseason roster for a time. Let's just not talk about his DRA, or that homer rate, or all the "at least he can't bat this time" barbs following his pre-Fall Classic demotion. Workman is who he is at this point—a serviceable and unremarkable middle relief arm—but it's nice to see him healthy, happy and with another ring.

YEAR	TEAM	LVL	AGE	WHIP	ERA	DRA	WARP	MPH	FB%	WHF	CSP
2016	PME	AA	27	2.20	9.00	5.07	0.0				
2017	PAW	AAA	28	1.00	1.55	3.30	0.6				
2017	BOS	MLB	28	1.21	3.18	3.68	0.7	94.7	51.4	11.3	45.9
2018	PAW	AAA	29	0.87	3.90	3.28	0.6				
2018	BOS	MLB	29	1.21	3.27	6.21	-0.6	93.2	38.9	11.1	48.1
2019	BOS	MLB	30	1.39	4.62	4.91	0.1	93.1	44.1	11.2	47

Brandon Workman, continued

Pitch Shape vs LHH

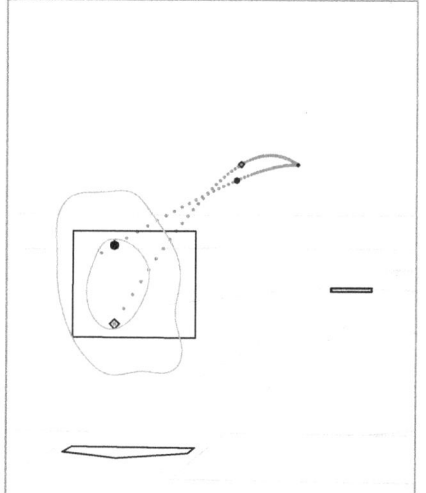

Pitch Shape vs RHH

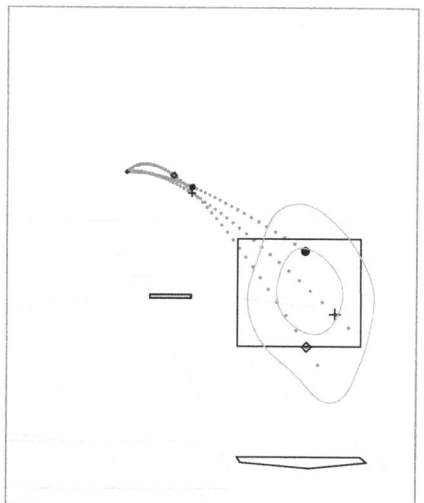

Type	Frequency	Velocity	H Movement	V Movement
● Fastball	38.9%	91.6 [97]	-3 [117]	-14.1 [105]
☐ Sinker				
+ Cutter	24.4%	86.9 [89]	4.2 [114]	-28.6 [80]
▲ Changeup				
✕ Splitter				
▽ Slider				
◇ Curveball	36.7%	80.8 [109]	5.6 [91]	-53.1 [89]
✥ Slow Curveball				
✷ Knuckleball				
▼ Screwball				

Steven Wright RHP

Born: 08/30/84 Age: 34 Bats: R Throws: R
Height: 6'2" Weight: 215 Origin: Round 2, 2006 Draft (#56 overall)

YEAR	TEAM	LVL	AGE	W	L	SV	G	GS	IP	H	HR	BB/9	K/9	K	GB%	BABIP
2016	BOS	MLB	31	13	6	0	24	24	156^2	138	12	3.3	7.3	127	46%	.279
2017	BOS	MLB	32	1	3	0	5	5	24	40	9	1.9	4.9	13	43%	.365
2018	PAW	AAA	33	0	0	0	5	3	16^2	20	0	2.2	4.9	9	48%	.333
2018	BOS	MLB	33	3	1	1	20	4	53^2	41	5	4.4	7.0	42	54%	.243
2019	BOS	MLB	34	1	1	0	19	0	20^1	19	2	3.7	7.0	16	46%	.287

Breakout: 9% Improve: 33% Collapse: 15% Attrition: 15% MLB: 77%
Comparables: Doug Fister, Jamey Wright, Whitey Ford

Wright saw such limited MLB action in 2018 for two reasons: recovery from offseason knee surgery and a 15-game suspension for violating MLB's domestic violence policy. Per reporting from NBCSB's Evan Drellich and others, Wright was arrested at his Tennessee home in December 2017 and charged with domestic assault and preventing a 9-1-1 call. The case was later retired in court, and charges will be dropped if Wright goes a year without another incident. "It's really hard on a personal level to get past something that's constantly being thrown at you," Wright said. "But I did it to myself. It's one of those things that I've got to live with the consequences that came from my actions that night." Wright was effective when on the field, and figures to have a chance to carve out a role on the 2019 Red Sox assuming he can recover from yet another offseason knee procedure. If he does, any success he enjoys should be framed as yet another example of a team making on-field success their top priority.

YEAR	TEAM	LVL	AGE	WHIP	ERA	DRA	WARP	MPH	FB%	WHF	CSP
2016	BOS	MLB	31	1.24	3.33	3.22	3.8	87.7	13.9	11.2	48.6
2017	BOS	MLB	32	1.88	8.25	8.93	-0.9	86.9	8.2	7.2	48.3
2018	PAW	AAA	33	1.44	3.78	5.13	0.0				
2018	BOS	MLB	33	1.25	2.68	2.72	1.5	87.8	6.1	10	52.3
2019	BOS	MLB	34	1.37	4.61	4.91	0.1	86.6	10.6	10.2	49.3

Steven Wright, continued

Pitch Shape vs LHH

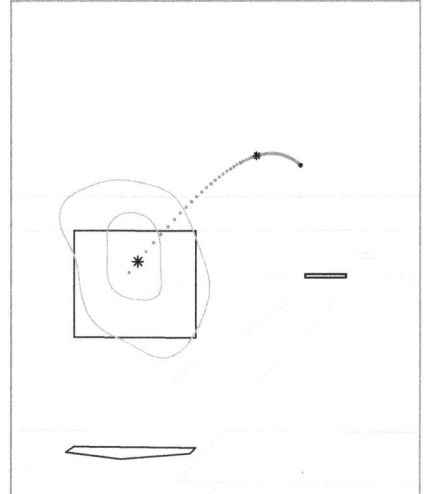

Pitch Shape vs RHH

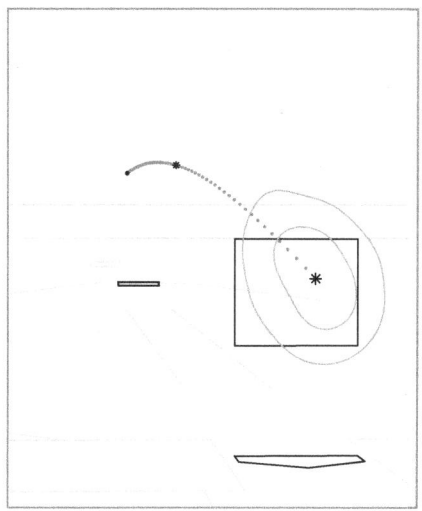

Type		Frequency	Velocity	H Movement	V Movement
●	Fastball	3.5%	85.6 [78]	-6 [103]	-18.4 [92]
□	Sinker	2.5%	82.7 [51]	-11.2 [111]	-27 [78]
+	Cutter				
▲	Changeup	1.7%	81.6 [85]	-10.9 [102]	-29.7 [93]
×	Splitter				
▽	Slider	0.4%	76.3 [64]	1 [83]	-31.7 [104]
◇	Curveball	1.5%	73.1 [80]	5.8 [92]	-57.6 [78]
✤	Slow Curveball				
✳	Knuckleball	90.4%	75.8 [111]	0.3 [111]	-42.6 [89]
▼	Screwball				

Triston Casas 3B
Born: 01/15/00   Age: 19   Bats: L   Throws: R
Height: 6'4"   Weight: 238   Origin: Round 1, 2018 Draft (#26 overall)

Lots of things went right for Casas in 2018. He hit .385/.545/.884 with seven homers as a senior at American Heritage School in Florida. He was drafted 26th overall by the Red Sox in June. He signed a $2.55 million bonus, gave an adorable interview on MLB Network and got to visit Fenway for the first time. Are you waiting for the other shoe to drop? Here it is: just two games into his GCL career, Casas tore the UCL in his right thumb diving for a ball, meaning he was SOL for the rest of the season. While hand injuries can be scary for hitters, there shouldn't be any long-term ramifications for Casas. He still profiles as a plus-power hitter who's willing to go the other way, as well as a defender who's perhaps more likely to become a good first baseman than average across the diamond. Assuming he fully recovers, it should be fun to see which reliever Dave Dombrowski trades him for in three years.

Rusney Castillo CF

Born: 07/09/87 Age: 31 Bats: R Throws: R
Height: 5'9" Weight: 195 Origin: International Free Agent, 2014

YEAR	TEAM	LVL	AGE	PA	R	2B	3B	HR	RBI	BB	K	SB	CS	AVG/OBP/SLG
2016	BOS	MLB	28	8	4	1	0	0	0	0	3	0	0	.250/.250/.375
2016	PAW	AAA	28	429	55	20	5	2	34	24	68	9	3	.263/.309/.354
2017	PAW	AAA	29	369	52	22	0	15	43	11	51	14	2	.314/.350/.507
2018	PAW	AAA	30	511	56	31	0	5	59	29	80	13	7	.319/.360/.416
2019	BOS	MLB	31	251	30	11	1	6	24	8	50	5	2	.266/.299/.391

Breakout: 0%   Improve: 22%   Collapse: 4%   Attrition: 28%   MLB: 45%
Comparables: Lou Montanez, Jason Bourgeois, Jason Pridie

Castillo is best known as a cautionary tale; an eight-figure international signee who has to date backfired more or less entirely. But is that really fair? In the four-plus years since Castillo signed with Boston, he's received 337 PA in the majors, and just eight of those have come since 2015. Castillo has proven definitively that he's too good for Triple-A, winning the International League batting title last season after thriving in 2017. So why no call up? Castillo's $10 million-plus AAV would count against the $237 million luxury tax threshold the Sox were desperately trying to stay under, at least until they splurged on Ian Kinsler in July. So why no call-up then? Perhaps because the Sox's four main outfielders consist of two MVP candidates, a 24-year-old stud and one of the game's best defenders. The Red Sox don't need and "can't afford" Castillo, but he's earned another shot to play in the big leagues. It's just unlikely to come in Boston.

YEAR	TEAM	LVL	AGE	PA	DRC+	VORP	BABIP	BRR	FRAA	WARP
2016	BOS	MLB	28	8	70	0.2	.400	0.4	LF(2): -0.5, CF(1): 0.0	0.0
2016	PAW	AAA	28	429	107	13.1	.310	4.6	CF(86): 10.1, LF(8): -1.8	2.5
2017	PAW	AAA	29	369	143	29.5	.332	3.0	CF(73): 4.7, RF(7): 0.6	3.1
2018	PAW	AAA	30	511	133	27.5	.372	1.2	CF(97): -4.6, RF(8): -0.4	2.3
2019	BOS	MLB	31	251	89	5.7	.315	0.0	CF 2, RF 0	0.8

Boston Red Sox 2019

C.J. Chatham SS

Born: 12/22/94 Age: 24 Bats: R Throws: R
Height: 6'4" Weight: 185 Origin: Round 2, 2016 Draft (#51 overall)

YEAR	TEAM	LVL	AGE	PA	R	2B	3B	HR	RBI	BB	K	SB	CS	AVG/OBP/SLG
2016	RSX	RK	21	25	2	2	0	1	2	0	7	0	0	.167/.200/.375
2016	LOW	A-	21	121	19	4	1	4	19	8	20	0	1	.259/.319/.426
2018	GRN	A	23	80	13	6	1	0	9	3	14	1	1	.307/.329/.413
2018	SLM	A+	23	392	42	14	1	3	43	21	72	10	4	.315/.355/.384
2019	BOS	MLB	24	251	19	5	0	6	24	6	65	2	1	.183/.205/.279

Breakout: 13%   Improve: 18%   Collapse: 0%   Attrition: 18%   MLB: 18%
Comparables: Yadiel Rivera, Angel Chavez, Blake Davis

Listen, pretty much anyone who lives in New England knows to associate Chatham with delays and late arrivals, but C.J. here was taking that connection to the extreme. Boston's second-round pick from 2016 missed a ton of time in 2017 with leg issues and hit the DL last season thanks to a viral infection. That's the bad news. The good news? Whenever he's been on the field, Chatham has hit. Sure, High-A shouldn't be a super challenging environment for a 23-year-old with college experience, but Chatham showed good bat-to-ball skills and a strong approach at the plate. Combine that with solid-to-good shortstop defense and you get the makings of a second-division starter or solid backup infielder. That probably makes Chatham a top-10 Red Sox prospect right now, which...yikes.

YEAR	TEAM	LVL	AGE	PA	DRC+	VORP	BABIP	BRR	FRAA	WARP
2016	RSX	RK	21	25	45	-1.4	.188	-0.1	SS(7): -0.3	-0.1
2016	LOW	A-	21	121	111	5.0	.282	-0.7	SS(26): 0.3	0.3
2018	GRN	A	23	80	120	1.6	.371	0.6	SS(4): -0.2	0.2
2018	SLM	A+	23	392	110	16.4	.380	2.7	SS(67): -3.6	0.8
2019	BOS	MLB	24	251	24	-14.4	.220	-0.4	SS -2	-1.8

Michael Chavis 3B

Born: 08/11/95 Age: 23 Bats: R Throws: R
Height: 5'10" Weight: 216 Origin: Round 1, 2014 Draft (#26 overall)

YEAR	TEAM	LVL	AGE	PA	R	2B	3B	HR	RBI	BB	K	SB	CS	AVG/OBP/SLG
2016	GRN	A	20	312	30	11	3	8	35	22	74	3	1	.244/.321/.391
2016	SLM	A+	20	27	5	0	0	0	1	2	7	1	0	.160/.222/.160
2017	SLM	A+	21	250	50	17	2	17	55	19	57	1	0	.318/.388/.641
2017	PME	AA	21	274	39	18	0	14	39	20	56	1	0	.250/.310/.492
2018	PME	AA	22	139	23	7	0	6	17	13	35	3	1	.303/.388/.508
2018	PAW	AAA	22	34	8	3	0	2	7	1	12	0	0	.273/.294/.545
2019	BOS	MLB	23	34	3	1	0	1	4	2	10	0	0	.188/.235/.312

Breakout: 12% Improve: 27% Collapse: 5% Attrition: 14% MLB: 44%
Comparables: Alex Liddi, J.D. Davis, Paul DeJong

When he was on the field in 2018, Chavis was pretty good. He continued to show promising game power and a willingness to take walks as he ascended the MiLB ladder, and he maintained an acceptable strikeout rate for good measure. But back to that "on the field" part... The oft-injured Chavis opened the year on the DL with an oblique issue. He had plenty of time to heal at least, as he was suspended 80 games for PED usage shortly thereafter. Chavis has more red flags than you like to see from a first-rounder, especially one with a likely defensive home at first. Still, his bat should make him a second-division starter or platoon corner bat at worst, and there's still some first-division upside if you squint. Though if the whole baseball thing *doesn't* work out, his status as a short, injury-prone steroid user could perhaps make him the next great Patriots receiver!

YEAR	TEAM	LVL	AGE	PA	DRC+	VORP	BABIP	BRR	FRAA	WARP
2016	GRN	A	20	312	98	13.2	.303	1.3	3B(68): -0.4	0.4
2016	SLM	A+	20	27	40	-0.8	.222	1.1	3B(2): -0.7	-0.1
2017	SLM	A+	21	250	170	28.8	.360	1.3	3B(27): -1.6	1.9
2017	PME	AA	21	274	104	12.0	.265	0.1	3B(43): -0.5, SS(1): 0.0	0.2
2018	PME	AA	22	139	145	13.3	.383	0.5	3B(18): 1.5, 1B(11): -0.5	1.0
2018	PAW	AAA	22	34	91	4.7	.368	0.2	3B(4): -1.2, 1B(1): 0.0	-0.1
2019	BOS	MLB	23	34	46	-1.4	.260	-0.1	3B 0	-0.2

Bobby Dalbec 3B

Born: 06/29/95   Age: 24   Bats: R   Throws: R
Height: 6'4"   Weight: 225   Origin: Round 4, 2016 Draft (#118 overall)

YEAR	TEAM	LVL	AGE	PA	R	2B	3B	HR	RBI	BB	K	SB	CS	AVG/OBP/SLG
2016	LOW	A-	21	143	25	13	2	7	33	9	33	2	2	.386/.427/.674
2017	GRN	A	22	329	48	15	0	13	39	36	123	4	5	.246/.345/.437
2018	SLM	A+	23	419	59	27	2	26	85	60	130	3	1	.256/.372/.573
2018	PME	AA	23	124	14	8	1	6	24	6	46	0	0	.261/.323/.514
2019	BOS	MLB	24	251	25	10	0	11	33	15	99	0	0	.193/.248/.377

Breakout: 12%   Improve: 30%   Collapse: 12%   Attrition: 26%   MLB: 52%
Comparables: Matt Chapman, J.D. Davis, Dylan Cozens

As fun as this would be, it probably isn't going to work out. Dalbec struck out in about a third of his plate appearances last year despite spending the bulk of the season as a 23-year-old in High-A. Yes, he has prodigious power and yes, Dalbec's glove and arm are up to the task at third base. But when your swing-and-miss generates more energy than the Gansu Wind Farm, the utility of your other tools tends not to matter so much. Only four qualified hitters K'd in more than 30 percent of their plate appearances last year, and of that whiff-happy quartet, only two—Joey Gallo and former Sox prospect Yoan Moncada—had even moderately productive seasons. Those are the odds Dalbec is up against, but if we know anything about him, at the very least he'll go down swinging.

YEAR	TEAM	LVL	AGE	PA	DRC+	VORP	BABIP	BRR	FRAA	WARP
2016	LOW	A-	21	143	213	19.0	.473	1.3	3B(22): 2.5	1.9
2017	GRN	A	22	329	112	12.9	.383	-2.0	3B(67): -2.3	0.4
2018	SLM	A+	23	419	160	44.2	.318	0.9	3B(91): 5.2, SS(1): 0.0	3.8
2018	PME	AA	23	124	96	7.1	.377	-0.1	3B(18): -3.9, 1B(2): -0.3	-0.4
2019	BOS	MLB	24	251	65	-5.4	.274	-0.6	3B 0, 1B 0	-0.6

Josh Ockimey 1B

Born: 10/18/95   Age: 23   Bats: L   Throws: R
Height: 6'1"   Weight: 215   Origin: Round 5, 2014 Draft (#164 overall)

YEAR	TEAM	LVL	AGE	PA	R	2B	3B	HR	RBI	BB	K	SB	CS	AVG/OBP/SLG
2016	GRN	A	20	499	60	25	1	18	62	88	129	3	1	.226/.367/.425
2017	SLM	A+	21	425	56	20	2	11	63	66	110	1	4	.275/.388/.438
2017	PME	AA	21	121	12	7	0	3	11	17	33	0	0	.272/.372/.427
2018	PME	AA	22	376	43	19	2	15	56	59	112	0	1	.254/.370/.473
2018	PAW	AAA	22	105	10	2	0	5	15	11	37	1	0	.215/.305/.398
2019	BOS	MLB	23	251	28	10	1	10	32	30	86	0	0	.210/.304/.397

Breakout: 11%   Improve: 24%   Collapse: 4%   Attrition: 20%   MLB: 37%
Comparables: Ryan Lavarnway, Travis Shaw, Ike Davis

Do you miss the big beefy sluggers of the early '90s? A time when half the first basemen in the league grew trucker goatees and couldn't field or run a lick but could hit the ball a country mile? If so, Ockimey is the throwback prospect for you. He does one thing and one thing well. He hits the ball very hard. And the ball subsequently travels very far. His prodigious raw pop plays on account of a decent approach, and that combination is the reason that Ockimey remains on the periphery of general baseball prospectdom despite no other discernible tools. For every one of these guys who turns into Jesus Aguilar there are dozens who never make meaningful progress past Double-A. That being said, Ockimey has already reached Pawtucket as a 22-year-old, so he doesn't just have power on his side; he's got time, too.

YEAR	TEAM	LVL	AGE	PA	DRC+	VORP	BABIP	BRR	FRAA	WARP
2016	GRN	A	20	499	132	23.0	.284	1.8	1B(101): -3.2	1.1
2017	SLM	A+	21	425	146	21.7	.362	-0.7	1B(91): -2.6	1.3
2017	PME	AA	21	121	124	2.6	.368	-0.5	1B(24): 0.2	0.2
2018	PME	AA	22	376	133	16.8	.339	-1.1	1B(71): -2.1	0.9
2018	PAW	AAA	22	105	85	-1.6	.294	-0.9	1B(20): -1.2	-0.4
2019	BOS	MLB	23	251	93	2.0	.289	-0.4	1B -1	0.1

Boston Red Sox 2019

Dustin Pedroia 2B

Born: 08/17/83 Age: 35 Bats: R Throws: R
Height: 5'9" Weight: 175 Origin: Round 2, 2004 Draft (#65 overall)

YEAR	TEAM	LVL	AGE	PA	R	2B	3B	HR	RBI	BB	K	SB	CS	AVG/OBP/SLG
2016	BOS	MLB	32	698	105	36	1	15	74	61	73	7	4	.318/.376/.449
2017	BOS	MLB	33	463	46	19	0	7	62	49	48	4	3	.293/.369/.392
2018	BOS	MLB	34	13	1	0	0	0	0	2	1	0	0	.091/.231/.091
2019	BOS	MLB	35	323	36	15	1	6	34	32	41	3	2	.286/.359/.408

Breakout: 0% Improve: 18% Collapse: 17% Attrition: 10% MLB: 87%
Comparables: Mark Loretta, Red Schoendienst, Frankie Frisch

We always knew this might happen. The aging curve for second basemen is notoriously unkind, and knee injuries are scary for any player—nevermind one who puts his knees in jeopardy with every double play he turns. But this is *Dustin Freakin Pedroia* we're talking about here. The dude played through a torn UCL in 2013 and hit .301! Surely through sheer force of will he'd find a way to buck the trend, to beat the odds, to hit .290 and play Gold Glove defense until he was 50 on one damn leg if he had to. Unfortunately, Father Time doesn't care how scrappy you are. Pedroia played in just three games last year, his October 2017 knee cartilage restoration surgery ultimately necessitating July 2018 arthroscopic surgery to clean up scar tissue. Despite turning 35 a month after his latest procedure, Pedroia vowed to be ready to play come Spring Training. Hopefully, he can make good on that promise, as Pedroia deserves to go out on his own terms. But it's clear that the Red Sox need to count any production they glean from Pedroia moving forward as a bonus, even as he's due $40 million over the final three years of his extension.

YEAR	TEAM	LVL	AGE	PA	DRC+	VORP	BABIP	BRR	FRAA	WARP
2016	BOS	MLB	32	698	120	26.4	.339	-2.0	2B(152): -2.7	3.3
2017	BOS	MLB	33	463	109	9.4	.315	-5.7	2B(98): -0.1	1.3
2018	BOS	MLB	34	13	97	-1.3	.100	-0.1	2B(3): -0.4	0.0
2019	BOS	MLB	35	323	113	15.1	.319	-0.6	2B -1	1.5

Durbin Feltman   RHP
Born: 04/18/97   Age: 22   Bats: R   Throws: R
Height: 6'0"   Weight: 205   Origin: Round 3, 2018 Draft (#100 overall)

YEAR	TEAM	LVL	AGE	W	L	SV	G	GS	IP	H	HR	BB/9	K/9	K	GB%	BABIP
2018	GRN	A	21	0	1	3	7	0	7	6	0	1.3	18.0	14	43%	.429
2018	SLM	A+	21	1	0	1	11	0	12¹	12	0	2.9	10.9	15	58%	.364
2019	BOS	MLB	22	1	1	0	24	0	25	23	3	4.4	9.5	27	44%	.302

Breakout: 7%   Improve: 10%   Collapse: 1%   Attrition: 8%   MLB: 11%
Comparables: Danny Barnes, Jacob Rhame, Ryan Burr

After Feltman enjoyed a successful college career as TCU's closer, Boston popped the undersized right-hander with the 100th-overall selection last June. Armed with a 60-grade slider and 70-grade fastball, Feltman carved up low minors hitters with ease in limited action. His performance didn't come as much of a surprise, and there's not much development left here; Feltman looks ready to challenge MLB hitters sooner rather than later. As Boston's relievers stumbled down the stretch, there were whispers that the Sox might fast-track Feltman to help their beleaguered bullpen. That didn't come to pass, but assuming he stays healthy, he could log significant innings in the 2019 Red Sox bullpen once their depth is tested.

YEAR	TEAM	LVL	AGE	WHIP	ERA	DRA	WARP	MPH	FB%	WHF	CSP
2018	GRN	A	21	1.00	2.57	1.65	0.3				
2018	SLM	A+	21	1.30	2.19	2.64	0.3				
2019	BOS	MLB	22	1.43	3.89	4.33	0.2				

Jay Groome LHP

Born: 08/23/98 Age: 20 Bats: L Throws: L
Height: 6'6" Weight: 220 Origin: Round 1, 2016 Draft (#12 overall)

YEAR	TEAM	LVL	AGE	W	L	SV	G	GS	IP	H	HR	BB/9	K/9	K	GB%	BABIP
2017	LOW	A-	18	0	2	0	3	3	11	5	0	4.1	11.5	14	58%	.208
2017	GRN	A	18	3	7	0	11	11	44^1	44	6	5.1	11.8	58	55%	.355
2019	*BOS*	*MLB*	*20*	*2*	*3*	*0*	*8*	*8*	*32^1*	*32*	*4*	*5.7*	*8.7*	*31*	*45%*	*.310*

Breakout: 0% Improve: 2% Collapse: 1% Attrition: 1% MLB: 3%
Comparables: Timothy Melville, Michael Kopech, Anthony Swarzak

When it comes to developing pitching prospects, the Red Sox are seemingly always the Groomsman and never the Groome. Our protagonist here was supposed to change all that after he was popped 12th overall in the 2016 draft, largely falling that far because of signability concerns. But pitching prospects have their own acronym for a reason, and two-plus years later, injuries and ineffectiveness have conspired to push Groome closer to "lottery ticket" than "blue-chipper" on the prospect scale. His recovery from mid-May Tommy John surgery figures to keep him off the mound for a solid portion of 2019. If he doesn't look sharper and healthier upon his return, he may not register on said prospect scale at all.

YEAR	TEAM	LVL	AGE	WHIP	ERA	DRA	WARP	MPH	FB%	WHF	CSP
2017	LOW	A-	18	0.91	1.64	3.33	0.2				
2017	GRN	A	18	1.56	6.70	3.80	0.8				
2019	*BOS*	*MLB*	*20*	*1.63*	*4.93*	*5.21*	*0.1*				

Darwinzon Hernandez LHP

Born: 12/17/96 Age: 22 Bats: L Throws: L
Height: 6'2" Weight: 245 Origin: International Free Agent, 2013

YEAR	TEAM	LVL	AGE	W	L	SV	G	GS	IP	H	HR	BB/9	K/9	K	GB%	BABIP
2016	LOW	A-	19	3	5	0	14	14	48^1	39	1	6.7	10.8	58	51%	.304
2017	GRN	A	20	4	5	0	23	23	103^1	85	8	4.3	10.1	116	50%	.292
2018	SLM	A+	21	9	5	0	23	23	101	80	1	5.3	11.0	124	46%	.326
2018	PME	AA	21	0	0	0	5	0	6	6	0	9.0	15.0	10	36%	.429
2019	BOS	MLB	22	1	1	0	2	2	10	10	1	7.4	9.4	10	42%	.295

Breakout: 7% Improve: 8% Collapse: 3% Attrition: 11% MLB: 12%
Comparables: Jimmy Barthmaier, Jose Cisnero, Dellin Betances

For the ever-growing segment of the interneting baseball world that loves itself some good-ass names, Hernandez is a prospect to keep an eye on. The latest in a line of flame-throwing Venezuelan lefties to bless Boston's farm system, Hernandez boasts a mid-90s fastball with natural cut and run that should be murder on his fellow southpaws. Secondary offerings include a changeup that needs development, a slider that needs development, and...uh...a curveball that needs development. Add his control and command to the list, too, but all those imperfections didn't stop Hernandez from striking out a ton of guys in High-A, Double-A and the AFL. Hernandez has likely evolved into Boston's best pitching prospect, and while his ceiling may be only a mid-rotation piece, his floor is also solid as a wicked weapon out of the 'pen. That's not bad for a guy the Sox signed for a cool $7,500 back in 2013.

YEAR	TEAM	LVL	AGE	WHIP	ERA	DRA	WARP	MPH	FB%	WHF	CSP
2016	LOW	A-	19	1.55	4.10	3.71	0.9				
2017	GRN	A	20	1.30	4.01	3.71	1.9				
2018	SLM	A+	21	1.39	3.56	4.91	0.5				
2018	PME	AA	21	2.00	3.00	2.35	0.2				
2019	BOS	MLB	22	1.80	5.35	5.94	-0.1				

Tanner Houck RHP

Born: 06/29/96 Age: 23 Bats: R Throws: R
Height: 6'5" Weight: 210 Origin: Round 1, 2017 Draft (#24 overall)

YEAR	TEAM	LVL	AGE	W	L	SV	G	GS	IP	H	HR	BB/9	K/9	K	GB%	BABIP
2017	LOW	A-	21	0	3	0	10	10	22^1	21	0	3.2	10.1	25	49%	.333
2018	SLM	A+	22	7	11	0	23	23	119	110	11	4.5	8.4	111	50%	.298
2019	BOS	MLB	23	5	7	0	19	19	83^2	87	11	4.9	7.5	69	43%	.302

Breakout: 5% Improve: 11% Collapse: 5% Attrition: 11% MLB: 16%
Comparables: Max Fried, Jimmy Barthmaier, Mike Hinckley

Boston's first-round pick in 2017, Houck had an okay first full professional season in 2018. He still needs to develop his changeup if he wants to stick in the rotation, but scouting reports indicate he's made progress with his slider, and his heavy low-to-mid-90s fastball remains a potent weapon. There's a chance his lack of a third pitch and delivery conspire to push him to the bullpen, at which point he could be ready for the majors quickly. There's also a chance his ideal frame, lively fastball and makeup allow him to emerge as a mid-rotation arm. It's not the highest-ceiling profile, but it's one of the best in the Red Sox system—though that may say more about the organization than it does about Houck himself.

YEAR	TEAM	LVL	AGE	WHIP	ERA	DRA	WARP	MPH	FB%	WHF	CSP
2017	LOW	A-	21	1.30	3.63	3.32	0.5				
2018	SLM	A+	22	1.43	4.24	5.61	-0.4				
2019	BOS	MLB	23	1.58	5.13	5.42	0.1				

Travis Lakins RHP

Born: 06/29/94 Age: 25 Bats: R Throws: R
Height: 6'1" Weight: 180 Origin: Round 6, 2015 Draft (#171 overall)

YEAR	TEAM	LVL	AGE	W	L	SV	G	GS	IP	H	HR	BB/9	K/9	K	GB%	BABIP
2016	SLM	A+	22	6	3	0	19	18	91	111	8	3.6	7.8	79	41%	.355
2017	SLM	A+	23	5	0	0	7	7	38	32	2	3.1	10.2	43	44%	.309
2017	PME	AA	23	0	4	0	8	8	30^1	34	2	6.2	5.6	19	48%	.337
2018	PME	AA	24	2	2	1	26	6	38	27	3	3.1	9.9	42	48%	.250
2018	PAW	AAA	24	1	0	2	10	0	16^1	11	0	2.8	8.3	15	44%	.244
2019	BOS	MLB	25	1	1	0	14	0	15	14	2	4.1	8.9	15	42%	.295

Breakout: 8% Improve: 13% Collapse: 2% Attrition: 11% MLB: 18%
Comparables: Daniel McCutchen, Parker Bridwell, Luke Farrell

For years, scouts worried that Lakins' lean frame and injury history would conspire to force him to the bullpen. That fear became reality, as the Sox finally shifted Lakins into a relief role last June. The good news? Lakins was flat out dominant in his new role, striking out more than a batter per inning in Double-A thanks in part to an uptick in velo. He thrived in a shorter sample against Triple-A hitters, too. There probably isn't closer upside here, but if he stays healthy—and that's a very big if—Lakins could emerge as a mid-to-late-inning weapon for the Red Sox as soon as May or June.

YEAR	TEAM	LVL	AGE	WHIP	ERA	DRA	WARP	MPH	FB%	WHF	CSP
2016	SLM	A+	22	1.62	5.93	4.61	0.9				
2017	SLM	A+	23	1.18	2.61	3.59	0.7				
2017	PME	AA	23	1.81	6.23	5.20	0.0				
2018	PME	AA	24	1.05	2.61	3.74	0.6				
2018	PAW	AAA	24	0.98	1.65	4.40	0.1				
2019	BOS	MLB	25	1.39	3.97	4.39	0.1				

Bryan Mata RHP

Born: 05/03/99 Age: 20 Bats: R Throws: R
Height: 6'3" Weight: 160 Origin: International Free Agent, 2016

YEAR	TEAM	LVL	AGE	W	L	SV	G	GS	IP	H	HR	BB/9	K/9	K	GB%	BABIP
2016	DRX	RK	17	4	4	0	14	14	61	54	2	2.8	9.0	61	51%	.319
2017	GRN	A	18	5	6	0	17	17	77	75	3	3.0	8.6	74	53%	.333
2018	SLM	A+	19	6	3	0	17	17	72	58	1	7.2	7.6	61	59%	.292
2019	BOS	MLB	20	3	5	0	13	13	59	62	7	6.5	7.1	47	49%	.306

Comparables: Kohl Stewart, Duane Underwood, Tyler Matzek

The pessimist looks at Mata's 2018 line and thinks there's absolutely no way someone with this type of command profile can be a starter. The optimist looks past Mata's unsightly walk rate and sees a 19-year-old who just put up a good ERA in High-A despite having less control over his offerings than a slot machine. Mata has a good fastball and an advanced changeup for a pitcher his age, and he draws praise for his sequencing and feel for pitching. None of that will matter if Mata's K:BB rate remains close to flat, but time is on his side, and the general consensus is that he retains mid-rotation upside.

YEAR	TEAM	LVL	AGE	WHIP	ERA	DRA	WARP	MPH	FB%	WHF	CSP
2016	DRX	RK	17	1.20	2.80	2.25	2.3				
2017	GRN	A	18	1.31	3.74	5.45	-0.1				
2018	SLM	A+	19	1.61	3.50	5.01	0.3				
2019	BOS	MLB	20	1.78	5.70	6.03	-0.4				

Michael Shawaryn RHP

Born: 09/17/94 Age: 24 Bats: R Throws: R
Height: 6'2" Weight: 200 Origin: Round 5, 2016 Draft (#148 overall)

YEAR	TEAM	LVL	AGE	W	L	SV	G	GS	IP	H	HR	BB/9	K/9	K	GB%	BABIP
2017	GRN	A	22	3	2	0	10	10	53^1	44	5	2.2	13.2	78	42%	.331
2017	SLM	A+	22	5	5	0	16	16	81^1	71	10	3.9	10.1	91	34%	.289
2018	PME	AA	23	6	8	0	19	19	112^2	100	7	2.2	7.9	99	40%	.287
2018	PAW	AAA	23	3	2	0	7	6	36^2	30	6	2.7	8.1	33	34%	.247
2019	BOS	MLB	24	1	1	0	2	2	10	10	2	3.3	8.2	9	36%	.294

Breakout: 13% Improve: 27% Collapse: 18% Attrition: 31% MLB: 55%
Comparables: Yefrey Ramirez, Thomas Pannone, Adam Plutko

Not every pitching prospect is a potential future ace. Most of them profile more like Shawaryn: a guy who could be a back-end starter, a medium-leverage reliever or the type of multi-inning swingman with whom some of the league's more innovative teams are exploring the space. Shawaryn's main weapons are a low-to-mid 90s sinking fastball that induces a lot of weak grounders in spite of poor command, and a slider that could break its way to a plus grade. He's strong and sturdy, having thrown nearly 300 innings in two-plus seasons since being drafted. But his three-quarters delivery is high-stress, lending further credence to the notion that his future may be in the 'pen. He's already succeeded in Triple-A, and Shawaryn seems a safe bet to make the majors in some capacity. We just might not know in what role for a while.

YEAR	TEAM	LVL	AGE	WHIP	ERA	DRA	WARP	MPH	FB%	WHF	CSP
2017	GRN	A	22	1.07	3.88	2.34	1.8				
2017	SLM	A+	22	1.30	3.76	3.76	1.4				
2018	PME	AA	23	1.13	3.28	4.12	1.6				
2018	PAW	AAA	23	1.12	3.93	3.21	1.0				
2019	BOS	MLB	24	1.40	4.79	5.32	0.0				

Boston Red Sox 2019

LINEOUTS

Hitters

HITTER	POS	TEAM	LVL	AGE	PA	R	2B	3B	HR	RBI	BB	K	SB	CS	AVG/OBP/SLG	DRC+	WARP
Juan Centeno	C	TEX	MLB	28	38	3	1	0	1	3	1	7	0	0	.162/.184/.270	81	0.0
	C	ROU	AAA	28	232	27	9	0	2	27	16	34	0	1	.234/.291/.307	65	-0.1
Danny Diaz	3B	DRX	Rk	17	113	17	7	0	6	27	5	27	0	3	.238/.283/.476	85	0.2
Jarren Duran	OF	LOW	A-	21	168	28	5	10	2	20	11	26	12	4	.348/.393/.548	168	1.6
	OF	GRN	A	21	134	24	9	1	1	15	5	22	12	6	.367/.396/.477	164	1.1
Antoni Flores	SS	DRX	Rk	17	57	10	3	1	1	14	8	7	0	1	.347/.439/.510	166	0.4
Brandon Howlett	3B	RSX	Rk	18	163	24	15	0	5	25	22	38	0	1	.307/.405/.526	187	0.9
Tzu-Wei Lin	SS	PAW	AAA	24	302	33	20	2	5	25	23	64	3	4	.307/.362/.448	130	2.1
	SS	BOS	MLB	24	73	15	6	1	1	6	8	17	0	1	.246/.329/.415	80	0.1
Tony Renda	INF	PME	AA	27	108	19	11	0	3	16	9	13	4	1	.371/.435/.577	170	0.7
	INF	PAW	AAA	27	184	30	8	1	2	11	11	31	6	1	.288/.337/.382	112	0.6

Last year's book brought up the fact that "Centeno" is Spanish for "Rye," but failed to point out that **Juan Centeno** plays catcher. So that means at one point, a scout pointed to Juan and thought: "There's a catcher in the Rye." ⓧ Boston's most recent second-round pick, **Nick Decker** is an athletic, bat-first, prep school outfielder from New Jersey who...oh my god did the Red Sox just get the next Mike Trout? ⓧ One of Boston's big-ticket J2 signings from 2017, **Danny Diaz** has begun his transformation from lithe shortstop to big beefy third basemen. He was pretty bad in the DSL, but he's younger than the 21st century, so he's got time. ⓧ Even by the most generous estimates, Duran Duran had about eight major hits. **Jarren Duran**, Boston's seventh-round pick, had 101 between Salem and Greenville in his surprisingly potent professional debut. ⓧ A six-figure J2 signing out of Venezuela in 2017, **Antoni Flores** draws praise for his defensive chops at short, his advanced feel for hitting and his projectable body. He stands out from other Red Sox prospects in that he actually has some upside. ⓧ Utility man **Marco Hernandez** now has more shoulder surgeries (three) than homers (one) over the past two seasons. He's still on a better run than Felix Doubront, at least. ⓧ After falling to 640th overall in the 2018 draft, **Brandon Howlett** took his anger out on Rookie-ball pitchers, savaging them to the tune of a 128 DRC+. He's a steady defender with a decent enough arm at third, but he lacks a true Howlett-zer. ⓧ **Tzu-Wei Lin** logged time at second, short, third and center field for the Red Sox and Paw Sox, officially making him Brock Holt's faster understudy. ⓧ You think *you're* tired of the Yankees and the Red Sox? The formerly formidable **Adam Lind** was released by the two rivals three times last season amidst hitting like a pitcher in Triple-A, if they were permitted to hit. ⓧ The Red Sox signed athletic Dominican outfielder **Eduardo Lopez** to a $1,150,000 contract as part of their 2018 J2 class. He was born on May 8, 2002. You, person reading this, are old.

⓪ What can we say about **Tony Renda** that hasn't been said about a spare tire or a travel insurance policy? It's not the end of the world if you have to use him, but you'd sure rather not.

Pitchers

PITCHER	TEAM	LVL	AGE	W	L	SV	G	GS	IP	H	HR	BB/9	K/9	K	GB%	WHIP	ERA	DRA	WARP
Colten Brewer	ELP	AAA	25	3	4	3	37	0	48	40	3	2.8	11.8	63	56%	1.15	3.75	2.55	1.4
	SDN	MLB	25	1	0	0	11	0	9^2	15	0	6.5	9.3	10	50%	2.28	5.59	2.71	0.2
Kutter Crawford	GRN	A	22	5	4	0	21	21	112^1	104	6	2.7	9.6	120	41%	1.23	2.96	4.42	1.0
	SLM	A+	22	2	3	0	6	6	31^1	28	0	4.0	10.6	37	43%	1.34	4.31	3.96	0.5
Jhonathan Diaz	GRN	A	21	11	8	0	26	26	153	123	6	2.3	8.6	147	55%	1.06	3.00	4.46	1.3
Bobby Poyner	PAW	AAA	25	0	0	6	33	0	43	43	4	2.3	7.3	35	26%	1.26	3.14	5.35	-0.1
	BOS	MLB	25	1	0	0	20	0	22^1	22	4	1.2	9.7	24	34%	1.12	3.22	5.31	-0.1
Roniel Raudes	SLM	A+	20	2	5	0	11	11	54	58	2	3.2	5.8	35	37%	1.43	3.67	4.18	0.7
Alex Scherff	GRN	A	20	1	5	0	15	15	65	68	7	3.2	7.1	51	42%	1.40	4.98	5.08	0.1
Chandler Shepherd	PAW	AAA	25	7	10	0	25	25	129^2	142	13	2.4	7.4	107	43%	1.36	3.89	4.08	2.1
Josh Taylor	VIS	A+	25	1	2	5	14	0	16	16	1	2.8	11.2	20	45%	1.31	2.81	2.56	0.4
	PME	AA	25	2	5	8	33	0	35^2	42	1	4.5	9.3	37	54%	1.68	3.79	3.78	0.5
Marcus Walden	BOS	MLB	29	0	0	1	8	0	14^2	14	0	1.8	8.6	14	58%	1.16	3.68	3.18	0.3
	PAW	AAA	29	0	4	2	18	5	32^2	44	2	4.7	6.6	24	53%	1.87	4.96	4.36	0.3

For **Colten Brewer**, the bad news is that he's the 10th best reliever on the 40-man roster. The good news is that there's never been a better time to be the 10th best reliever on a 40-man roster. ⓪ You'll never guess what generic back-end starter prospect **Kutter Crawford**'s best secondary pitch is. ⓪ Statistically speaking, 84 percent of all Red Sox prospects are left-handed starters from Venezuela. **Jhonathan Diaz** is among that group, though he lacks the upside of some of his younger countrymen. ⓪ Large adult right-hander **Justin Haley** remains a little too good for Triple-A and a little too bad for the majors. If only there was a term for this type of player... ⓪ Potential future up-and-down reliever **Austin Maddox** threw just 7.2 professional innings as he battled right shoulder inflammation, proving that a single vowel isn't all that separates him from one of baseball's great pitching families. ⓪ When we last saw **Jenrry Mejia**, he was dealing as an elite late-game reliever back in 2014 and 2015. Since then, he's had three PED suspensions and has recently been reinstated from his lifetime ban from MLB. The only thing more questionable than his judgement is his future performance. ⓪ Prototypical LOOGY **Bobby Poyner** earned a surprise spot on the Opening Day roster, held opponents scoreless in four of his first six MLB appearances, and then got demoted to Triple-A anyway. He should probably get familiar with the Providence-to-Boston commuter rail line. ⚾ The Red Sox's farm system may not be great, but it's improved to the point where control artist/windup wonder **Roniel Raudes** isn't one of its best arms anymore. He added nearly as many DL stints (two) as quality starts (five) to his Salem resume in 2018. ⚾ Ok, close your eyes. Now imagine a non-elite hard-throwing righty pitching prospect from Texas. Congratulations, you just invented **Alex Scherff**! ⚾ We don't want to reduce **Chandler Shepherd**'s identity to that of a run-of-the-mill quad-A reliever, but let's just say that if he was a product, Costco would sell him in packs of 12. ⚾ **Josh Taylor** is left-handed enough that he was added to Boston's 40-man roster this offseason despite only occasionally knowing where the pitches he throws will be located. ⚾ When David Henry Thoreau writes about Walden Pond, it's inspirational. When we write about **Marcus Walden**, it's to let you know he doesn't miss enough bats.

Red Sox Prospects

The State of the System:
In hindsight, I should have ended this five month slog of research and writing with a better system, like… well… any of the other ones really.

The Top Ten:

1 Bobby Dalbec 3B OFP: 55 Likely: 45 ETA: 2020
Born: 06/29/95 Age: 24 Bats: R Throws: R Height: 6'4" Weight: 225
Origin: Round 4, 2016 Draft (#118 overall)

The Report: Two years ago, we ranked Dalbec as an other of note with the epithet "Possibly a better pitching prospect." Last year he slotted into the next ten and I made a strained milkshake duck joke about his swing and miss tendencies. This year he's the number one prospect in the system. I don't feel great about this, but I don't feel great about the Red Sox system generally. Dalbec achieved this ranking in part by becoming even more Bobby Dalbec than he was before. He just leaned into the whole profile, striking out, walking, or homering in over half of his plate appearances. He's Rob Manfred's worst nightmare.

Dalbec offers 70 raw power but it's unlikely to end up playing to full grade in the majors. In short, he's gonna strike out a lot. He has bat speed to spare, but the swing is grooved and he's vulnerable to hard stuff up sequenced with spin down. That's something major-league pitchers have in their locker. Dalbec is still taking the vast majority of his reps at third, and he's improved enough there to be passably averageish. As long as he continues to hit around .240-.250 and get those big bombs into games though, you won't care if he's a first baseman either.

The Risks: Medium. With this much swing-and-miss in play, it's just never gonna be low. Even if he hits in the upper minors this year.

Ben Carsley's Fantasy Take: I understand why Dalbec can be considered the best IRL prospect in this system, but he's a borderline top-150 dynasty prospect at best. I personally don't love his chances of bringing his prodigious power into games, and even if I'm wrong it's still a shade below the Joey Gallo brand of 40-plus homer potential. If you really love him, you're closing your eyes and hoping for something like the prime Mike Moustakas years offensively. That'd make Dalbec a useful but hardly irreplaceable fantasy piece, and again, that's his ceiling.

Boston Red Sox 2019

2. Michael Chavis 3B

OFP: 55   Likely: 45   ETA: 2019
Born: 08/11/95   Age: 23   Bats: R   Throws: R   Height: 5'10"   Weight: 216
Origin: Round 1, 2014 Draft (#26 overall)

The Report: After serving an 80-game suspension for testing positive for a banned substance, Chavis picked up where he left off in 2017 as a three-true-outcomes slugger. Chavis has 70 raw pop derived from plus bat speed and a big uppercut, but the swing can get long and only really has one gear. Chavis knows balls and strikes well enough, but he has a prominent hole up in the zone which major-league arms may exploit. How much of his power he gets into games will ultimately shape his major-league role, as the hit tool will likely play fringe at best, and he's a below-average third baseman.

Chavis moves well enough at the hot corner, and he's sneaky athletic despite a bit of a beer-keg physique, but the arm is fringy and he especially struggles throwing on the move. He started to play more first base in 2018, and the power might carry the profile even on the right side of the infield. Still, an R/R first base profile is a tough sell unless there's clear plus regular upside.

The Risks: Moderate, which is higher than you'd like from a corner bat profile in the upper minors. Chavis doesn't offer a ton outside of the light tower power, so if he can't get it into games consistently, or stick at third base, he's a tough fit on a modern roster.

Ben Carsley's Fantasy Take: I fully understand why Chavis isn't the best IRL prospect in this system, but he *is* the best dynasty prospect in the system. That being said, he was still only in the 90s in our Top 101. You'd usually list a future in Boston as a positive with a hitting prospect, but Chavis' best bet at fantasy relevancy may be as a second-division starter on a worse team. If he gets to 500 or so PA, he could challenge for 30 homers a year, hopefully while retaining 3B eligibility throughout his 20s. If he stays on the Red Sox, he may end up as a short-side platoon bat, and it's tough to care about those guys in mixed leagues no matter how much power they have.

3. Triston Casas 1B

OFP: 55   Likely: 45   ETA: 2022
Born: 01/15/00   Age: 19   Bats: L   Throws: R   Height: 6'4"   Weight: 238
Origin: Round 1, 2018 Draft (#26 overall)

The Report: It's almost like the Red Sox have a type. Casas is another corner slugger—this one of the more hulking variety—albeit one a fair bit further from the majors than Dalbec or Chavis. He also suffered a season-ending thumb injury in his second pro game. When you are drafting a prep first baseman in the first round, you naturally expect game-changing power in the tool shed, and it's not hard to see where Casas gets his prodigious raw pop. The swing has length and uppercut and he's a big, strong kid.

The long term question—as it always is for this profile—is how much of that raw power will get into games. It's not the world's most athletic swing, and the bat speed is only solid-average, so he's gonna be riskier than Dalbec and Chavis even irrespective of the distance from the majors. Casas played third base in high school, and his one pro game for the Sox was at the hot corner, but it's unlikely they'll roll him out there forever. His long term home will be first base.

The Risks: High.

Ben Carsley's Fantasy Take: Bret ranked Casas at 21 on his Top 50 2019 signees list, and that seems fair to me. Casas is almost certainly a first baseman, which isn't great, but he has more fantasy upside than, say, Pavin Smith did a year ago. He's probably a top 200 dynasty prospect right now, though closer to the end of that list than the front half.

4

Tanner Houck RHP   OFP: 55   Likely: 45   ETA: 2020
Born: 06/29/96   Age: 23   Bats: R   Throws: R   Height: 6'5"   Weight: 210
Origin: Round 1, 2017 Draft (#24 overall)

The Report: Houck didn't exactly hold up his end of the bargain as the kind of quick-moving first-round college arm the Sox probably thought they popped in 2017. There's several markers here that suggest he will be better suited to the pen long term. The delivery is funky and high effort, with a bit of crossfire and a low-three-quarters slot. He has struggled to develop a third pitch, making him primarily a fastball/slurve guy. The fastball is easy plus though, touching the mid-90s with good run and sink.

Houck struggles to get consistent shape with his breaking ball, which tends to have more sweep than depth and overall slurvy break. He commands the pitch well enough, but it projects more as average or solid-average than a true bat-misser. He has an athletic, projectable frame, and was used about as heavily as any college arm will be in his first pro season, so durability is less of a concern w/r/t starting than… well, everything else. The sinking fastball is potentially good enough that he could be a very effective reliever though, even if he isn't one of the strikeout monsters we normally see in the late innings nowadays.

The Risks: Medium. The sinking fastball is enough to dispatch most of the hitters he will face in the minors, but there are profile risks given the delivery and lack of a third pitch.

Ben Carsley's Fantasy Take: Even if Houck does remain a starter, he lacks the type of strikeout stuff we need to have much interest from a fantasy POV. Honestly, his best odds at being of much use for our purposes will come if he emerges as a closer some day. Sadz.

5

Durbin Feltman RHP   OFP: 55   Likely: 45   ETA: Early 2019
Born: 04/18/97   Age: 22   Bats: R   Throws: R   Height: 6'0"   Weight: 205
Origin: Round 3, 2018 Draft (#100 overall)

The Report: Feltman was arguably the best college closer in the country this spring, and in his pro debut he looked like a dude you could drop right into a major-league pen. While not always working with his upper-90s velocity he showed in college, Feltman throws a plus fastball. He changes eye levels well with it. It shows good riding life up, and he can sink it down in the zone from his OTT slot. His power slider is a mid-80s monster that drops off the deck and is already plus. The delivery is very high effort, bordering on violent, but I mean, he's a reliever. It's not closer™ stuff at present, but if he starts touching 99 again, he could get there. Regardless he's about as safe a late-inning relief prospect as you'll find in the minors right now.

The Risks: Low. Feltman is a major-league ready reliever.

Ben Carsley's Fantasy Take: Between the 20-grade name and the fact that he'll only be fantasy-relevant if closing, Feltman is a dude you can avoid.

6. Jay Groome   LHP

OFP: 55   Likely: 40   ETA: 2021-22
Born: 08/23/98   Age: 20   Bats: L   Throws: L   Height: 6'6"   Weight: 220
Origin: Round 1, 2016 Draft (#12 overall)

The Report: On talent, Groome is clearly the best prospect in the system. He spins a potential 80-grade curve. He has a fastball that bumps into the mid-90s. He has an advanced changeup. He has a classic pitcher's frame and motion.

He's also becoming an advertisement for waiting a bit into a guy's pro career before drawing firm conclusions. After an abbreviated post-draft debut in 2016, Groome missed nearly half of 2017 with a lat problem. He did not pitch well when he did get on the mound, with inconsistent velocity and poor command. He didn't even make it to the regular season in 2018, injuring his elbow during spring training and ultimately undergoing Tommy John surgery in mid-May.

It's currently unclear when—or even whether—Groome will get on a mound in 2019. It's even less clear what it's going to look like when he does. Throw in the long-reported makeup concerns that we discussed last year, and it's hard to be terribly optimistic until and unless he gets back and throws well.

The Risks: Extreme, but also with positive risk if he finally gets healthy and gets it together.

Ben Carsley's Fantasy Take: Despite having done nothing but disappoint since being drafted, Groome is pretty clearly the best dynasty pitching prospect in this system. That may say more about the Sox's farm than it does Groome himself, but there's still top-of-the-fantasy rotation upside here. Groome is just very, very unlikely to reach it at this point.

7. Darwinzon Hernandez   LHP

OFP: 50   Likely: 40   ETA: 2020
Born: 12/17/96   Age: 22   Bats: L   Throws: L   Height: 6'2"   Weight: 245
Origin: International Free Agent, 2013

The Report: Hernandez is a lefty who sits around 95, so there's a pretty good chance he pitches in the bigs at some point. I would definitely lobby for a soccer-style use of the first name on the back of his jersey, as there were seven Hernandezes in the majors last year but only one Darwinzon knocking on the door. The 70-grade name here is better than any of his pitches, but the stuff is major-league-quality as well.

In addition to a plus fastball, Hernandez has an above-average, low-80s slider that tunnels well off the heater despite lacking big two-plane break. There's a slower curve as well for a different look (although it's far less consistent at present than the slider) and a changeup that flashes average as well. Hernandez has a compact arm action, but he has struggled to repeat it or throw strikes consistently throughout his pro career. The fastball/slider combo is enough to be a major league reliever—perhaps even in the late innings if his fastball bumps in short bursts—but even in that role he will have to find the plate more consistently to get past "frustrating middle-inning arm," even if the stuff should make him far better than that.

The Risks: Medium. It's mid-90s velocity from the left side. He's going to get chances.

Ben Carsley's Fantasy Take: If it seemed more likely that Hernandez could start, he'd be a potential top-150 dynasty prospect thanks to his strikeout potential. Unfortunately, Hernandez probably isn't a starter, so…

8 Bryan Mata   RHP   OFP: 50   Likely: 40   ETA: 2021
Born: 05/03/99   Age: 20   Bats: R   Throws: R   Height: 6'3"   Weight: 160
Origin: International Free Agent, 2016

The Report: Last year for Mata we wrote that "[he] can lose his release point and overthrow. He'll just lose the zone completely at times." 'At times' in 2017, became 'way too much of the time' in 2018. His release point got even more scattershot in 2018, although it was mostly of the alternating miss "armside and up and then down and away" variety. When Mata did find the zone, he touched 95 more consistently with some armside run from his three-quarters slot, a potentially average curveball, and an improving changeup. He just wasn't in the zone enough and had his season cut short by six weeks or so due to back stiffness. While I wouldn't go so far as to call it a lost year, it's certainly one he'll want to forget. The raw stuff is still there for a mid-rotation arm, and Mata doesn't turn 20 until a month into the season, but that projection seems further away now than it did a year ago.

The Risks: High. He walked seven per nine in A-ball and had back issues.

Ben Carsley's Fantasy Take: You think this is painful for you? I'm a Red Sox fan…

9. Michael Shawaryn RHP

OFP: 50   Likely: 40   ETA: 2019
Born: 09/17/94   Age: 24   Bats: R   Throws: R   Height: 6'2"   Weight: 200
Origin: Round 5, 2016 Draft (#148 overall)

The Report: Shawaryn's stuff won't pop off the page here, but he's a bulldog who goes after hitters and is a particularly tough at-bat for righties due to his funk and low armslot. He'll touch 95 with the fastball, but generally sits in the low-90s. The pitch is sneaky fast due to the deception in his delivery, and there's some natural gloveside run from his slot. The command and control are fringy, and he has trouble hitting his spots east-west.

Shawaryn shows a full four-pitch mix, but only the slider is worth writing home about. He gets better depth on it than you'd expect given his low-three-quarters slot, and he manipulates the shape and speed of the offering well. It will flash plus, but projects as average. Shawaryn will use a slower curve to steal a strike now and again, but it lacks a distinct shape and may just be further slider manipulation. The change lacks ideal velocity separation. It's generally too firm in the upper-80s, although it will flash enough fade at times for you to project it to at least have some major-league utility keeping lefties honest. There's a fair bit of effort in Shawaryn's delivery and the stuff will back up later in games, making a reliever outcome likely here.

The Risks: Medium. The stuff just might not play against major-league bats, but Shawaryn has little left to prove in the minors.

Ben Carsley's Fantasy Take: A back-end starter or reliever prospect who'll call Fenway home? Sorry, but most of these guys don't turn into Derek Lowe.

10. Nick Decker OF

OFP: 50   Likely: 40   ETA: 2023
Born: 10/02/99   Age: 19   Bats: L   Throws: L   Height: 6'0"   Weight: 200
Origin: Round 2, 2018 Draft (#64 overall)

The Report: Decker is the cold weather prep outfielder version of Dalbec, Chavis, and Casas. Okay, that's a bit of an unfair oversimplification. Decker has potential plus raw power due to his natural strength—dude looks good in the uniform—plus bat speed, and loft in the swing. The barrel control at present is a little loose, and it's gonna be a slow burn on the hit tool. The stick is going to need to get to average though, as Decker is likely to slide to right field in his twenties due to fringy range on the grass. A wrist injury limited him to just two games in the complex this summer, but this was going to take a while regardless.

The Risks: Extreme. Cold weather prep bat with only a complex league resume, and barely one at that. Tweener/positional questions.

Ben Carsley's Fantasy Take: Watch List City. At least he's not a budding middle reliever!

Others of note:

Josh Ockimey, 1B, Triple-A Pawtucket

One more corner slugger for the road perhaps? Ockimey is certainly one possible future for Triston Casas if the hit tool doesn't develop. He's not that far off the Dalbec and Chavis types either, except he is definitely a first baseman—and not a particularly good one—and has actualized less of his ample raw power in games. He's less athletic than any of the top three bats in the system and despite being the closest to the majors, ranks much further below them—although the distance here overstates the gap; this is a mushy system past the first five names or so.

The culprit here is a long swing and average bat speed. The swing and miss has gone up at every stop, and Ockimey struggles with same-side pitching and spin generally. He does have the long side of the platoon 1B/DH at least, but his bat is going to have to conquer Triple-A first, and as you will probably gather from the other 29 lists, this profile is disappearing from major-league benches.

Travis Lakins, RHP, Triple-A Pawtucket

One of the advantages of publishing the Boston list last on the website is we have a pretty good idea what their offseason has looked like. It makes those potential "Factors on the Farm" a bit more obvious. Well, Roster Resource currently lists their closer as a Rule of Two of Ryan Brasier and Matt Barnes. The only reliever they have added so far is Jenrry Mejia. So yeah, they could probably use some bullpen help.

Lakins might be exactly what they need. He took off after a conversion to the pen in 2018, riding a plus fastball/cutter combination to a late-season promotion to Pawtucket. He continued to miss bats in Triple-A, and there isn't really anything stopping him from staking a claim at a 2019 bullpen slot.

Boston Red Sox 2019

Top Talents 25 and Under (born 4/1/93 or later):

1. Andrew Benintendi
2. Eduardo Rodriguez
3. Rafael Devers
4. Bobby Dalbec
5. Michael Chavis
6. Triston Casas
7. Tanner Houck
8. Durbin Feltman
9. Jay Groome
10. Darwinzon Hernandez

There weren't many difficult calls here. The trio of Red Sox veterans are unambiguously ahead of the farmhands, whose ranks were noticeably thinned in an effort to bolster the big-league team in recent years; this is how a U25 list usually looks after a championship.

Benintendi has quietly developed into one of the league's best outfielders. Now, it's strange to use "quiet" here: we're talking about a former top prospect who just helped lead his team to a championship—in Boston no less. But the Arkansas product's well-rounded game, stoic demeanor, and linear big-league development path have pushed him further below the radar than other young stars of similar caliber. That shouldn't obscure Benintendi's emergence as a great player in his own right. He's an impact contributor on both sides of the ball, as capable of swaying a game at the plate as in the field. He'll be a perennial 20/20 threat well into the next decade, and I wouldn't bet against him winning a batting title or two, either.

By all measures, Rodriguez has pitched well for the Red Sox. He's been considerably above-average on a rate basis over the last two seasons, and he posted a tidy 3.77 DRA (84.2 DRA-) in 2018. Per traditional scouting convention, that makes him a low No. 2 or very good No. 3 starter.

Rodriguez is a man of his time though, and like many pitchers of his generation, he hasn't been pushed particularly hard: He's never started more than 24 games in his four big-league seasons, nor has he topped 140 innings. You can't really be a Role 70 player with that kind of workload—not with an ERA in the high 3's, anyway. Barring a significant acceleration in roster trends and innings management, "starting pitchers" aren't going away any time soon. But more and more of the good ones will have usage patterns that resemble how the Red Sox have handled Rodriguez.

Given that, you could argue Devers should slot second and I wouldn't put up much of a fight. We ranked him as our fifth best prospect in the midseason 2017 list, just three weeks before the Red Sox summoned him to Boston. He played well down the stretch that summer and appeared on the cusp of stardom.

Stardom may yet lie in Devers' future, but he didn't get any closer to reaching it in 2018. After a decent start, his bat cooled down in mid-May and never really got going again. He missed a few weeks on both sides of mid-August and was yanked in and out of the lineup against lefties (against whom he hit just .229/.272/.347). That, along with a few notably bad throwing errors, gives me pause. Devers still projects as an impact hitter, and if a seer told me tomorrow that one of he and Rodriguez was about to post a 5-WARP campaign in 2019, I'd assume it was the former. For now though, the southpaw seems more likely to be a good player this season.

Only two other big leaguers were considered here. Sam Travis hit his first big-league dinger last September, but he doesn't project as a regular and has little chance of finding consistent playing time in Boston. Tzu-Wei Lin hit his first homer in the same game as Travis, and his positional flexibility gives him a decent chance to be a Swiss Army knife off the bench. Both just missed the list; perhaps their World Series rings will help alleviate some of the disappointment.

Part 3: Featured Articles

The Hole in The Shift is Fixing Itself

Russell Carleton

I've been on a bit of a mission against The Shift of late. I'm not out to get The Shift for the usual reasons that people oppose it. The words "the right way to play the game" won't be found on my lips. If a team wants to pursue a strategy that is within the rules and it works, then by all means, they have my blessing (not that they need it). Instead, my concern with The Shift is a worry that it doesn't work, or at least that it has a flaw that needs fixing.

The data show that while The Shift does a decent job of preventing singles on balls in play (what it's supposed to do), it also increases the number of walks that happen in front of it, and the number of additional walks outweighs the number of singles saved. It's a problem because you can't throw a guy out if he gets to walk to first base.

But the "why" was important. It seemed that The Shift was changing the way in which pitchers pitched. We saw that there were fewer fastballs thrown in front of The Shift than we might otherwise expect, and that pitchers tended to stay out of the strike zone a little more. Not by a lot. In fact, it might not even be visible to the naked eye. The percentage of pitches that are out of the zone goes from 51.0 to 53.3 from a standard defense (two right/two left) to a full shift (three on one side). That difference stands up even after we control for the types of hitters that get shifted against. And it's enough to drive up the walk rate to where it cancels out the benefits that teams thought they were getting with The Shift... and then some.

But there was some hope. I found that when individual pitchers stayed closer to the in-zone/out-of-zone mix that they used without The Shift on, they could still get the benefits of The Shift without the walk problems. So, in theory, a team could simply figure out a way to convince its pitchers to not fall prey to the walk trap and The Shift would once again be their friend.

It's reasonable to think that some teams might be more hip to this idea than others. Maybe some figured it out a year before the others. Maybe they were better at getting the message across to their pitchers. Or, maybe no one has figured it out yet.

Warning! Gory Mathematical Details Ahead!

I used data from 2015-2017, made available through MLB's data portal, Baseball Savant. They are kind enough to note when teams are using an infield shift (three fielders on one side of second base), as opposed to a "strategic shift" (someone's playing a bit out of position, but it's not quite that drastic) or a "standard" alignment.

Since we're doing this by team, I can't just look at raw walk rates, because we know that some teams have good pitchers and others have not-so-good pitchers. Some have a mix of both. I used the log-odds ratio method to take into account a batter's general walking proclivities, and a pitcher's as well, and then shoving them into a binary logistic regression. Then, I asked the computer to generate a specific coefficient for each team's pitchers, for when they went into The Shift and how that affected their walk rate.

Using those coefficients, I was able to project what would happen if a league-average pitcher faced a league-average hitter (which we expect would produce a league-average walk rate; from 2015-2017, 7.7 percent of plate appearances ended in a walk) and then just switched his hat. Here's the top five and the bottom five:

Top 5 Teams	Projected Shift Walk Rate	Bottom 5 Teams	Projected Shift Walk Rate
Rockies	6.2%	Rangers	11.2%
Pirates	6.7%	Mets	10.4%
Indians	7.2%	Dodgers	10.2%
Astros	7.3%	Cardinals	9.9%
Braves	7.7%	Tigers	9.7%

There are probably people out there right now trying to figure out what the common thread is among the top and bottom teams. I'm sure, because this is Baseball Prospectus, people are already trying to make the case that sabermetric "early adopters" have some sort of edge here. I think that the more interesting piece is that by the time you get to fifth place in The Shift, we're at league average.

As a sanity check, I examined the issue on a pitch-by-pitch level, looking at how often pitchers threw their pitches in the GameDay strike zone, and again using the same basic methodology and getting team-specific coefficients. The names on the list re-arranged themselves, but the idea was the same, and the two lists correlated with an R of .593.

There's a reason that I don't usually do this type of leaderboard post. I don't really know what the Rockies, Pirates, Indians, Astros, and Braves have in common, or what they have that the bottom five don't. I can put a shrug emoji here and say, "Well, it must be something!" but that seems like a cop-out. Instead, I'd like to present another table and suggest that the table above doesn't even really matter anymore.

Year	League Percent Outside K Zone (Full Shift)	League Percent in K Zone (No Shift)	Difference
2015	54.1%	51.1%	3.0%
2016	53.3%	50.9%	2.4%
2017	52.6%	50.9%	1.7%
2018	52.0%	50.7%	1.3%

The hole in The Shift is fixing itself, and it's coming down really fast league wide. In my earlier work on The Shift, I suggested that until teams stopped having such a huge difference between their out-of-zone rate with and without The Shift on, there would just be too many walks for The Shift to make sense. It seems that all 30 of them have been working toward just that. I once estimated that it takes about 10 years for an idea to filter its way through baseball. At this rate, it looks like teams are going to catch up a lot faster than that. And yeah, they're all saber-smart now.

It's likely that whatever magic it was that the Rockies and Pirates had has made its way to Texas and Queens. Or is at least on its way. And if teams are committing to fixing the walk problem, then it's likely that they will continue shifting and shifting a lot.

And eventually it's going to actually make sense for them to do it.

—*Russell Carleton is a former author of Baseball Prospectus and now an analyst for the New York Mets.*

The State of the Quality Start

Rob Mains

One of the seven things you (probably) didn't know about the 2018 season is that quality starts—defined as a start lasting six or more innings with three or fewer earned runs allowed—as a percentage of total starts cratered to an all-time low of 41 percent. I want to look a little more deeply into this, since it's been a while (May of 2016, to be exact) since I've examined quality starts.

The term *quality start* is credited to *Philadelphia Inquirer* sportswriter John Lowe. It's been derided ever since he coined it in December of 1985. Three runs in six innings? That's a 4.50 ERA! In what world is that a measure of quality?

Let's start with that criticism. It's true that 3 x 9 / 6 = 4.5. (You came here for this sort of high-level math, right?) But it's also true that type of start, meeting the bare minimum for earning a quality start, is unusual. Here's the proportion of quality starts in which the pitcher lasted exactly six innings and yielded exactly three earned runs. (I'm going to confine this analysis to the 30-team era, 1998-present. Almost all data retrieved in this article is via the Baseball-Reference Play Index.)

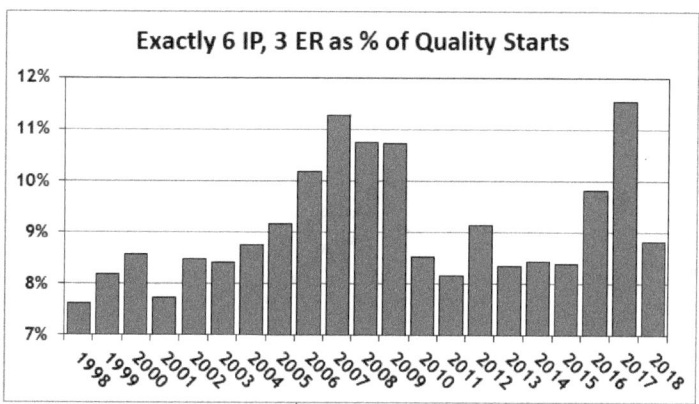

There were 1,997 quality starts in 2018. Only 176, or fewer than one in 11, featured a pitcher going six innings and allowing three earned runs. Put another way, the percentage of quality starts that resulted in a 4.50 ERA (8.8 percent) is less than half the percentage of games in which a batter hit two home runs and his team lost (22.5 percent; 237-69 won-lost). That doesn't impugn hitting two homers.

So if a 4.50 ERA isn't the norm, what is? How good are quality starts?

Pretty good, it turns out. First, on a team level:

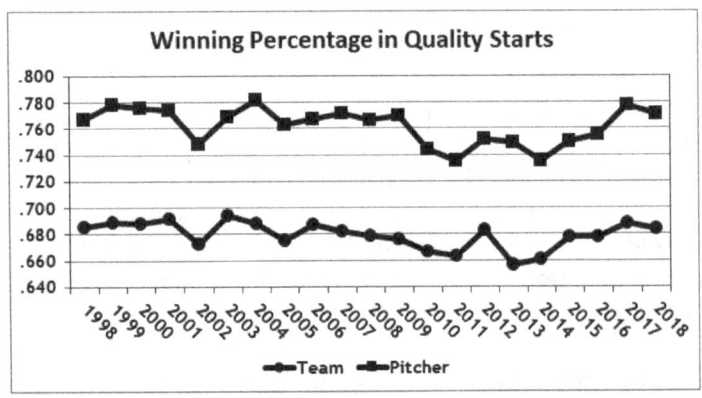

Teams receiving a quality start from their pitcher won 68.4 percent of their games in 2018, in line with the 30-team era average of 67.9 percent. A team with a .684 winning percentage wins 111 games. Getting a quality start is definitely a good thing. Individual pitchers throwing quality starts have a higher winning percentage because a big slice of team losses is assigned to a reliever.

If teams do well in quality starts, how well do the starting pitchers do? Again, very well.

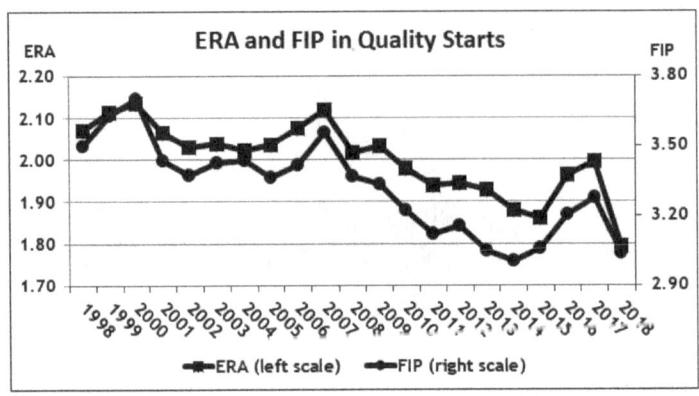

Pitchers in quality starts had a 1.79 ERA (blue line) in 2018, *the lowest in the 30-team era*. Their FIP was higher, 3.04, but still excellent. In the 30-team era, only 2014 had a lower FIP for quality starts, 3.01.

But, of course, the run environment in 2014 was different. Teams in 2014 scored 4.07 runs per game, the fewest in a non-strike year since 1976. They scored 4.45 runs per game in 2018. So surrendering a 3.04 FIP in 2018 is more impressive than 3.01 in 2014. Accordingly, let's look at ERA and FIP in quality starts relative to league averages.

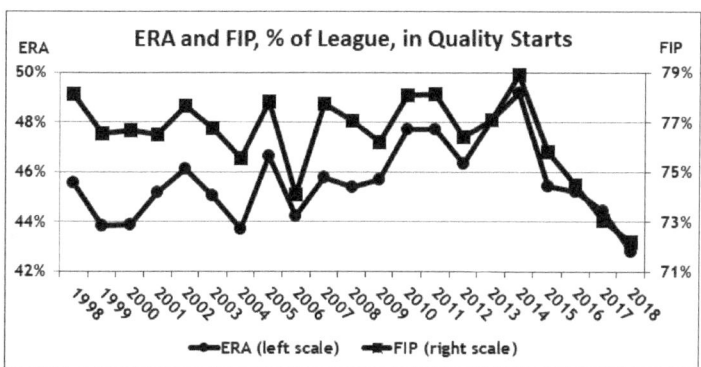

This tells a more dramatic story. Starting pitchers in 2018 gave up a 4.19 ERA and a 4.21 FIP. Starters in quality starts gave up a 1.79 ERA, 43 percent of the league average. Starters in quality starts gave up a 3.04 FIP, 72 percent of the league average. Both of these marks represent lows in the 30-team era.

The takeaway here is this: *Quality starts are better, relative to other starts, than they've ever been over the past 21 years.*

Maybe during the winter I'll look at this over a longer arc of time. For now, though, we can definitively say quality starts are the best they've ever been since the Diamondbacks and Rays joined the majors.

Yet, paradoxically, they're down.

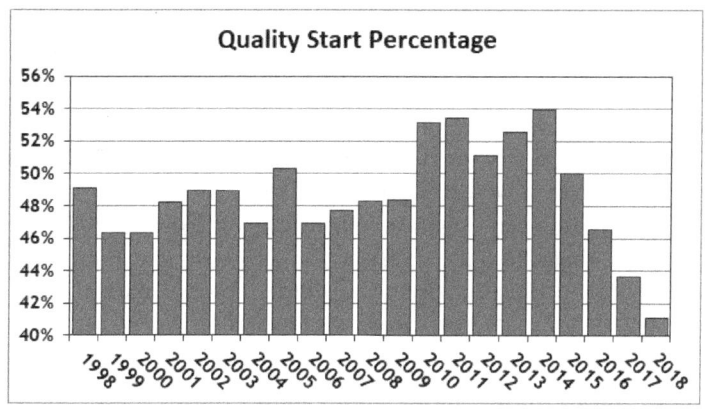

This graph covers only the 30-team era. In my article last week, though, I looked at the years 1908-2018. The result was the same. The 41 percent of starts in 2018 that were quality starts are an all-time low, well below the runners-up: 1930's 43 percent (the year teams scored an all-time record 5.55 runs per game) and last year's 44 percent.

The normal explanation for a dip in quality start percentage is an increase in scoring. When teams score a lot of runs, it's harder for starting pitchers to last six or more innings and limit opponents to three earned runs. From 1998 to 2014, the correlation between runs scored per game and the percentage of starts that were quality starts was -0.94. That means there was an extremely close relationship: More runs, fewer quality starts. Too small a sample? Go back to the start of the Expansion Era, 1961, and the relationship is even more negative, a -0.95 correlation, though 2014.

But that's broken down over the past four years:

- 2015: Runs per game increased from 4.07 to 4.25, quality start percentage decreased from 54.0 to 50.1. Yes, that's a negative relationship, but the regression model would predict a decline of 1.5 percentage points. We got 3.9 instead.
- 2016: Runs per game increased from 4.25 to 4.48, quality start percentage decreased from 50.1 to 46.6. Past experience would suggest a decline of just 1.8 percentage points. We got 3.4.
- 2017: Runs per game increased from 4.48 to 4.65, quality start percentage decreased from 46.6 to 43.6. Again, the direction's right, but the magnitude isn't. Using the relationship from 1998 to 2014, that increase in scoring should've reduced quality starts by 1.3 percentage points, not 2.9.
- 2018: Runs per game declined from 4.65 to 4.45. That should've resulted in the quality start percentage moving in the other direction, rising 1.6 points. It didn't. It fell 2.6 points, as noted, to an all-time low.

Granted, we're talking about just four years here. Maybe they're outliers. But I don't think they are. Quality starts, as noted, are as good or better than ever. But they're rarer than ever as well. And I think I know why.

To get a quality start, you need to allow three or fewer earned and pitch at least six innings. That's 18 outs. Here's a graph showing the number of starting pitchers who limited their opponents to three or fewer earned runs but got pulled after pitching at least five innings but fewer than six:

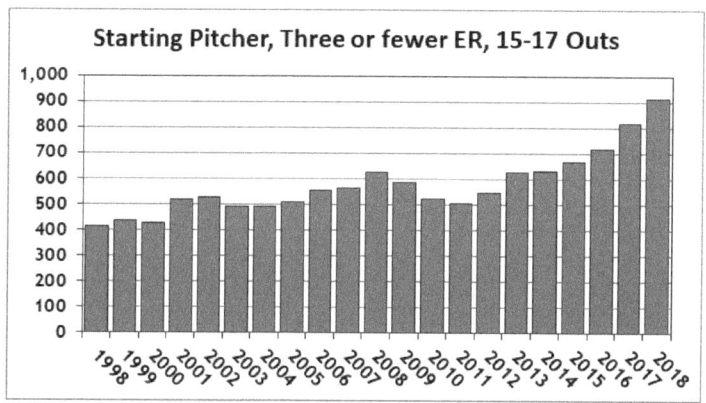

A pitcher getting 15 outs pitched five innings. A pitcher getting 16 outs pitched 5 1/3. A pitcher getting 17 outs pitched 5 2/3. More than ever before, pitchers are being removed from games in which they are within 1-3 outs of a quality start, falling just short of the six-inning finish line. Widespread acknowledgement of the times-through-the-order penalty and a flotilla of available bullpen arms is making the quality start simultaneously both more excellent and more rare.

Which is ironic, given that we saw a new post-war quality start record this season:

Rank	Pitcher	Season	Consecutive QS
1	Jacob deGrom	2018	24
2	Bob Gibson	1968	22
-	Chris Carpenter	2005	22
4	Johan Santana	2004	21
5	Luis Tiant	1968	20
-	Mike Scott	1986	20
-	Jake Arrieta	2015	20
8	Robin Roberts	1952	19
-	Tom Seaver	1973	19
-	Jack Morris	1983	19
-	Greg Maddux	1998	19
-	Josh Johnson	2010	19
-	Jon Lester	2014	19

While there have been longer streaks spread over multiple seasons, no pitcher since World War II threw more consecutive quality starts in one year than Jacob deGrom this year. The fact that he did in a year in which quality starts were the rarest they've ever been adds to the accomplishment.

—*Rob Mains is an author of Baseball Prospectus.*

Heads-Up Hacking—The First Pitch

Matthew Trueblood

Batters fell behind in a higher percentage of all plate appearances in 2018 than in any previous season for which we have pitch-by-pitch data. That kind of granular information goes back only to 1988, but we might safely assume (given all we know about baseball as it had been before that, and as it has been in the years since) that batters have *never* fallen behind at a higher rate than they did last season.

Through the 1990s, the percentage of all plate appearances that began 0-1 hovered in the high 30s and low 40s. In the 2000s, it rose steadily but slowly, through the mid-40s. In 2018, 49.8 percent of all trips to the plate began 0-1. That, as much as anything, captures in microcosm the nature of hitting in MLB today.

A countdown clock toward strike three begins ticking almost the moment a batter takes his place in the box. The league's adjusted OPS+ on the first pitch was higher in 2018 than ever before, and that has been true in most of the last 10 seasons. Batters hit .264/.289/.442 in all plate appearances in which they swung at the first pitch last season, and .241/.330/.395 in all plate appearances in which they took that first offering.

The percentage differences in batting average and isolated power there favor swinging at the first pitch by more than in any season since 1988, while the difference in on-base percentage favors taking by more than ever. If you want to get on base at a decent clip, it's a good idea to be patient, but you run the risk of missing the only chances you'll get to produce power.

Boston Red Sox 2019

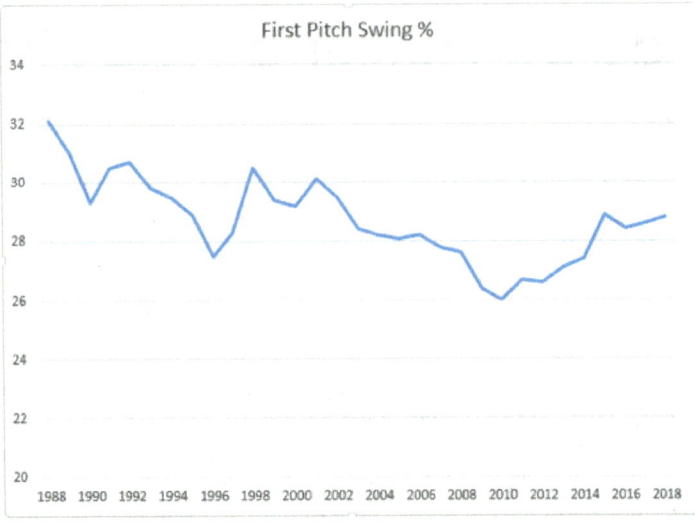

The league swung at the first pitch 28.8 percent of the time in 2018. With the isolated exception of 2015, that's the highest that number has climbed since 2002, but it might not be high enough. With the help of BP research maven Rob McQuown, I looked at the aggregate Called Strike Probability (CSProb) on the first pitch for each season since 2008, when the implementation of PITCHf/x first made measuring that possible. It's risen sharply during that period.

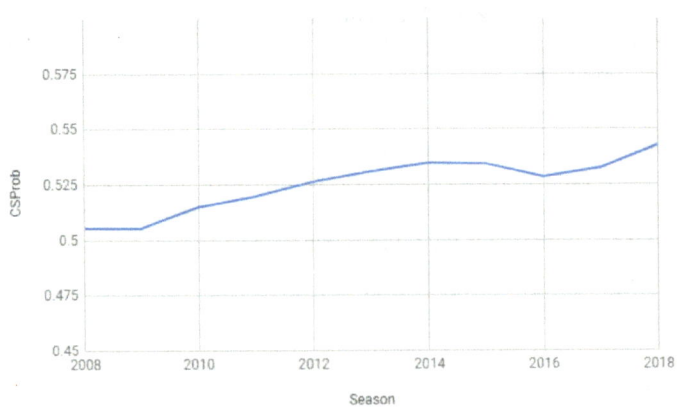

Called Strike Probability, First Pitch of PA (2008-2018)

Called Strike Probability is exactly what it sounds like: a pitch with a given CSProb has roughly that chance of being called a strike, if not swung at. In 2018, a batter who took 100 first pitches from a random sampling of the league's pitchers might expect to fall behind 54 or 55 times—up from 50 or 51 times in 2008. Almost regardless of pitch type (and, notably, especially in the case of fastballs), the first pitch tends to have more of the zone right now than ever before.

Pitchers are better at throwing strikes. They have better stuff, and believe more in their ability to miss bats within the zone. Perhaps most importantly, they know that batters are looking for one thing on the first pitch: a fastball. If they don't get it, they're likely to take the pitch. Check out how the use of sinkers and four-seamers on the first pitch has changed in a decade:

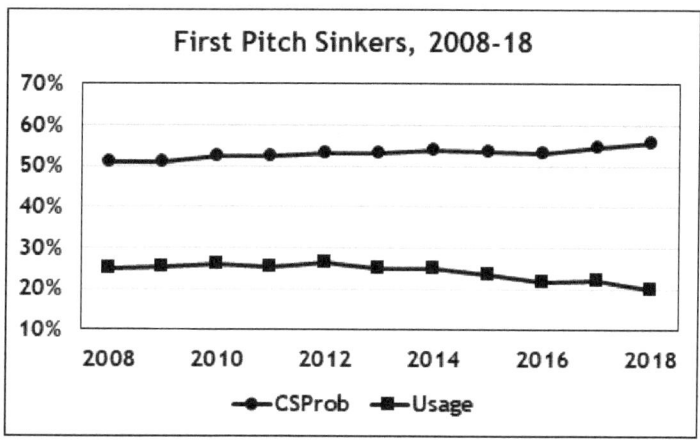

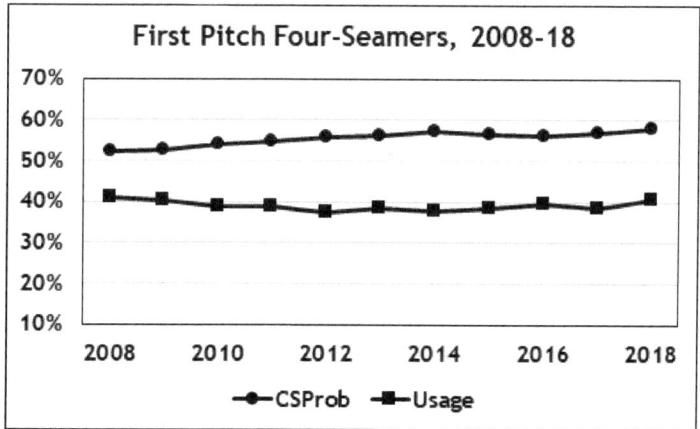

The sinker is losing its place in baseball, but the rate at which pitchers have thrown it on the first pitch hasn't dropped any faster than its usage rate in other counts. Pitchers have actually gone to their four-seamer *more* often to open counts, in the last few years, after a dip in the 2012-2015 period. What's really changed, though, and what shows up in both charts above, is that pitchers are catching more of the zone with first-pitch fastballs than they were a decade ago, or a half-decade ago. They're attacking right away, even with the pitch they know batters are expecting. The message is pretty clear: batters are being too passive.

Sliders, curves, and changeups each have more of the zone when thrown on the first pitch than they did several years ago, too, though the effect is less pronounced. Pitchers have seen the numbers; they know batters are doing better on the first pitch itself. They still feel safe throwing more and better strikes than ever before, figuring they'll come out ahead as long as they keep getting ahead to open each battle.

The Moneyball revolution brought an increased league-wide focus on OBP, which resulted in a de facto mandate to take a more patient tack at the plate. It worked very well for a while, as batters with poor plate discipline were compelled to either adjust or be expelled from the league, and pitchers with poor control were slowly weeded out.

However, concurrent with that revolution, and spurred by it in some ways, was the evolution of the pitching paradigm that now dominates the game. As batters ratcheted up their focus on inflating pitch counts and working walks, pitchers honed theirs on throwing strikes and missing bats. The league's understanding of what makes a good pitcher improved at least as much, from the mid-1990s through the mid-2000s, as its understanding of what makes a good hitter. As amphetamines and other performance-enhancing drugs were phased mostly out of the game, and as PITCHf/x broke onto the scene, individuals and teams learned how to exploit the evolved approaches of even the smartest hitters.

The ability to avoid making outs is still the most valuable one in baseball, but the magnitude of its eclipse of slugging is smaller than ever. To a greater extent than power, on-base skills derive their value from chaining—from the on-base skill levels of the players on either side of a given individual. Eleven years ago, when the housing crisis hit, people learned the hard way that the value of their homes depended a good deal on the values of their neighbors' homes. The same wasn't true, though, of their cars. So it is now, with OBP and SLG.

The global OBP in 2018 was .318. The only seasons since the Dead Ball Era in which the league got on base at a worse clip were 2013-2015, 1988, 1971-1972, and 1963-1968. This is all happening despite the aforementioned evolution of the science of hitting. It's happening despite a shift in approach and focus, one that would steer OBP ever higher, if only it were working.

Instead, it's sitting at a low ebb, and while it does so, even guys who get on base often are a little less helpful than they were 10 years ago—or 20, or 40, or 60, or 70, or 80, or 90. They're less helpful, that is, because unless there happen to be three or four other guys in the lineup who get on just as regularly, their contribution is merely to forestall the inevitable. Runs happen, increasingly, when a sudden bang happens, and that means attacking early in the count—because pitchers are sure as hell doing that.

In a league making contact on barely 75 percent of its swings, and a league in which an increasing number of pitchers can throw multiple off-speed pitches for strikes in any count, the only way to consistently generate offense is going to be aggressive. This isn't necessarily true for individuals, like Mookie Betts and Jose Ramirez, who make a lot of contact and have excellent plate discipline, and whose power comes from such natural quickness in a short stroke. Most players have to make tradeoffs, though, whether it be lowering their contact rate or raising their chase rate, in order to consistently make the quality of contact necessary to survive in today's game.

Highest %	Lowest %
Javier Baez – 48.3	Joe Mauer – 4.6
Freddie Freeman – 47.1	Mookie Betts – 9.7
Ozzie Albies – 46.3	Brett Gardner – 10.7
Jose Altuve – 44.2	Jose Ramirez – 12.0
Nick Castellanos – 44.1	Jason Kipnis – 13.8
Joey Gallo – 42.3	Jesus Aguilar – 14.5
Corey Dickerson – 40.9	Xander Bogaerts – 15.8
Salvador Perez – 40.8	Brian Dozier – 16.3
Eddie Rosario – 40.7	Mike Trout – 17.6
Nick Ahmed – 40.4	Yasmani Grandal – 17.6

Top 10 and Bottom 10 Hitters, First-Pitch Swing Rate (2018)

The question isn't which of these lists one prefers, but what they each convey, qualitatively, about the cat-and-mouse game of early-count hitting. Those top five on the left, especially, drive home the fact that for most players, getting aggressive early in the count is now key to keeping strikeout rate down and hitting for power.

For now, the message is: pitchers are coming right after batters with the nastiest stuff they've ever had. Batters had better stop giving away strike one and force hurlers to adjust, or the global OBP crisis is only going to get worse.

—*Matthew Trueblood is an author of Baseball Prospectus.*

A Hymn for the Index Stat

Patrick Dubuque

We survived without computers. I know this, because I remember the day when my dad hooked up his brand-new Atari 400 computer to the back of our 12-inch Magnavox television, and the perfect blue of the memo pad lit up for the first time. I was born just on the edge of that transitional generation, of learning cursive and balancing checkbooks and just doing math all the time, constant manual arithmetic.

It still amazes me. We learned how to sail ships without computers. We learned how to do calculus. We built towers that didn't fall down, most of the time. We engineered catapults to knock them down anyway. We built a robust system of philosophy called "utilitarianism," founded on the principle that the good of an action is evaluated by summing the effects of that action, which is the kind of formula that would make the world's mainframes crash. The whole foundation of statistics as a field is "here's math you could easily do but would die of old age first."

The fact of the matter is that there is too much math in the world to do. There are too many things changing, and too many things too small to notice, for us to handle. At some point, they become too much for the computers to handle as well, which is why we have chaos theory and undetectable earthquakes, but it's not an even fight. At some point, we fall back on intuition, and given how under-equipped we are, we're forced to bestow that intuition with some sort of supernatural superiority, the "gut feeling," that we can't prove because we can only intuit that our intuition is better.

We're all lousy at intuition, and wonderful at lying to ourselves about it. The honest truth is that computers are far better at intuition than we are, because in order to know what feels "off" you have to know what's "on." In order to do that you have to constantly reassess the average of everything, then re-rank your own experience against it.

Test your own, by comparing these three anonymous lines:

Player	G	HR	AVG	OBP	SLG
Player A	156	38	.259	.342	.535
Player B	154	38	.280	.348	.527
Player C	158	38	.266	.343	.509

These all seem like pretty similar players, right? The second one a touch more batted-ball dependent, the third a little less strong, but all pretty good hitters. And you'd be right, about the latter. Not the former.

Here's the breakdown:

- Player A: 1991 Howard Johnson, 141 DRC+
- Player B: 1996 Dean Palmer, 121 DRC+
- Player C: 2018 Giancarlo Stanton, 114 DRC+

Baseball is fortunate to have escaped the seismic shifts of so many other sports, where the talents and performances of other eras are nearly unrecognizable. (And not just other sports: try to explain the greatness of the movie Duck Soup without adjusting for era.) But they're still there, and they're nearly impossible to account for manually, without having to resort to sweeping generalizations like "steroid era" or juiced-ball era" to throw out entire swathes of production.

This is all to say that we should celebrate the index stat, that simple 100-based scale with such a humble aim: just to give context. It's hard to imagine how we lived without them for so long. Sabermetricians have always tried to make their stats look like other stats: True Average mapped to batting average, FIP molded to look like and compare to ERA. It's easy to understand the motivation—these statistics carry an emotional value in them that is hard to resist, as with the .300 hitter and the 2.00 ERA—but even they fall prey to the same loss of scale as their unadjusted counterparts. If a .300 average means different things in different years, does that hold true for a .300 True Average?

Instead, 100 doesn't say anything, except above average or below. And it does it instantly, for every season in every run environment for any statistic we want it to. We should have more index stats: K%+, so we can stop comparing Mike Clevinger's career 9.46 K/9 to Nolan Ryan's 9.55. HBP%+, so we can note that Ron Hunt was getting plunked when nobody else was getting plunked, as opposed to that imitator Brandon Guyer. Some might note how stale these references are and accuse league-adjustment as a backward-looking drive, and this is true. But we're always looking backward, always comparing the new with the expectations already set. The index stat just forces us to be honest.

There's always resistance to a new statistic, especially one so outwardly simple and so internally complex. We tend to stick with what we know, even in the case of formulas that are supposed to tell us what we know. But if your resistance is that it seems too complicated, too counterintuitive, too "black boxy," I encourage you to consider why you feel that way. Because the real world is infinitely more complicated than baseball, where all the pitches go in one basic direction and the baserunners are only allowed to travel in four directions. Baseball statistics based on mixed methodology are almost impossibly intricate. So are skyscrapers and automobiles. That's why we have computers—to take the guesswork out of them.

—*Patrick Dubuque is an author of Baseball Prospectus.*

Index of Names

Barnes, Matt	50	Leon, Sandy	34
Benintendi, Andrew	20	Lin, Tzu-Wei	94
Betts, Mookie	22	Martinez, J.D.	36
Bogaerts, Xander	24	Mata, Bryan	92, 101
Bradley, Jackie	26	Moreland, Mitch	38
Brasier, Ryan	52	Nunez, Eduardo	40
Brewer, Colten	95	Ockimey, Josh	85, 103
Casas, Triston	80, 98	Pearce, Steve	42
Castillo, Rusney	81	Pedroia, Dustin	86
Centeno, Juan	94	Porcello, Rick	60
Chatham, C.J.	82	Poyner, Bobby	95
Chavis, Michael	83, 98	Price, David	62
Crawford, Kutter	95	Ramirez, Erasmo	64
Dalbec, Bobby	84, 97	Raudes, Roniel	95
Decker, Nick	102	Renda, Tony	94
Devers, Rafael	28	Rodriguez, Eduardo	66
Diaz, Danny	94	Sale, Chris	68
Diaz, Jhonatan	95	Scherff, Alex	95
Duran, Jarren	94	Shawaryn, Michael	93, 102
Eovaldi, Nathan	54	Shepherd, Chandler	95
Feltman, Durbin	87, 99	Smith, Carson	70
Flores, Antoni	94	Swihart, Blake	44
Groome, Jay	88, 100	Taylor, Josh	95
Hembree, Heath	56	Thornburg, Tyler	72
Hernandez, Darwinzon	89, 100	Travis, Sam	46
Hernandez, Gorkys	30	Vazquez, Christian	48
Holt, Brock	32	Velazquez, Hector	74
Houck, Tanner	90, 99	Walden, Marcus	95
Howlett, Brandon	94	Workman, Brandon	76
Johnson, Brian	58	Wright, Steven	78
Lakins, Travis	91, 103		

Ballpark diagrams for Baseball Prospectus are created by THIRTY81Project, a design concept offering original ballpark artwork, including the new 'Ballparks of 2019' 11 x 17 color print.

Visit **www.thirty81project.com** for full details.